P9-DBQ-551

Borzoi Books ON LATIN AMERICA

General Editor
LEWIS HANKE
COLUMBIA UNIVERSITY

*The Conflict
Between Church and State
in Latin America*

THE
Conflict Between
Church and State
IN
Latin America

Edited with an Introduction by

FREDRICK B. PIKE

UNIVERSITY OF PENNSYLVANIA

New York: Alfred A. Knopf

NOTE: *Several selections in this book, as indicated in the source footnotes, were not available in English translation. These have been translated by Fredrick B. Pike, who wishes to acknowledge with thanks the assistance he received from Gonzalo Cartagenova and Rafael Torrella in preparing them.*

L. C. catalog card number: 64-10793

THIS IS A BORZOI BOOK,
PUBLISHED BY ALFRED A. KNOPF, INC.

FIRST EDITION

FIFTH PRINTING, AUGUST 1967

DEDICATED TO

J. LLOYD MECHAM,

whose work on Church and State in
Latin America has been the foundation
on which all subsequent studies
have been built.

Contents

III. THE CONTEMPORARY SCENE

*The Conflict
Between Church and State
in Latin America*

Introduction

IN 1947, José María Caro, then Cardinal-Archbishop of Santiago, Chile, denounced a Chilean political party because, in part, of its outspokenly critical attitude toward the Franco administration in Spain. In 1949, Costa Rica's Archbishop Víctor Manuel Sanabria y Martínez lashed out against a proposed article for the new constitution then being formulated which declared that education was essentially a function of the state. The archbishop's flat assertion that the Church would not accept this concept even if it were to be embodied in the new constitution helped bring about the defeat of the proposal. In 1954, the opposition of the Catholic Church was a contributing factor to the overthrow of Guatemala's communist-infiltrated Jacobo Arbenz administration. The following year the Church in Argentina gave its support to the uprising that toppled the régime of Juan Domingo Perón, a man whose presidential bid the Church had overtly supported in 1946. By the beginning of 1958, Marcos Pérez Jiménez and Gustavo Rojas Pinilla had been forced out of office in Venezuela and Colombia respectively, and in both instances Church opposition probably hastened the end of their dictatorial régimes. Perón had been engaged for some time in a bitter struggle with the Church. Both Pérez Jiménez and Rojas Pinilla, however, appeared to be anxious to maintain friendly relations between Church and state. Interestingly enough, both the Vatican and the State Department in Washington seemed to decide at about the same time that their respective interests might no longer be served by supporting friendly dictators who were intransigently dedicated to preserving the *status quo* against mounting pressure for social change.

In the above examples of recent participation in Latin American political affairs, as well as in others, the Roman Catholic Church has acted in accordance with its traditionally asserted right to serve as the final arbiter of issues which affect the moral and spiritual well-being of peoples who, either actually or nominally, are overwhelmingly Catholic. Church insistence upon the exercise of this right has frequently led to difficulties in Latin America, where individualistic Catholic laymen are apt to consider themselves competent to make moral judgments free from clerical influence. Even if the lay faithful are willing to accept the authority of the Church in the spiritual realm, friction can result from the fact that churchmen claim the power to define what constitutes moral and spiritual issues. Matters which some churchmen regard as having moral and spiritual implications are often considered by lay political leaders as purely political and secular in nature and therefore removed from the Church's competence.

The roots of the long-enduring conflict between clerical and anticlerical forces in Latin America reach into earliest colonial times. From almost the outset of the Spanish conquest of America, relations between Church and state were governed by the *patronato real*, or the system of royal patronage. By 1508 the principal powers and privileges involved in royal patronage had already been bestowed upon the Spanish crown, primarily by a papal bull issued in that year by Pope Julius II. The most important power accruing to the crown from the system of royal patronage was the right of nomination to Church benefices in the "Indies."

The system of royal patronage, augmented by traditional Spanish patterns of royal control over ecclesiastical affairs as well as by the gradually expanding claims of royal authority which the Vatican was in no position to contend, produced unique results. The Church in Spanish America was, from an administrative point of view, more a Spanish, national Church, controlled from Madrid, than a Catholic Church, controlled from Rome. The "Catholic Kings" Ferdinand and Isabella opposed Pope Alexander VI when in 1493 he sought to send a papal *nuncio* to the island of Española. After seeking unsuccessfully to find a permanent compromise to the issue, the Pope yielded to the royal wishes, and not until the early nineteenth century did a direct agent of the papacy set foot in Spanish America.

The control which the Spanish kings were able to exercise over the Church in the Indies has been summarized in the following terms by the distinguished Mexican historian Joaquín García Icazbalceta:

By virtue of the bull of Julius II and of other concessions subsequently secured, the Spanish kings came to exercise a power in the ecclesiastical government of America which, except in purely spiritual matters, appeared to be pontifical. Without the king's permission, no church, monastery, or hospital could be constructed and no bishopric or parish erected. No priest or friar might go to America without his express license. The kings named bishops and, without waiting for their confirmation by the pope, sent them out to administer their dioceses. The kings marked out the boundaries of the bishoprics and changed them at their pleasure. They could appoint to any religious office— even to that of sacristan—if they wished. They had the power to reprove severely, to recall to Spain, or to banish any ecclesiastical official, including bishops who, even though they might often dispute with governors, never failed to listen to the voice of the king. The kings administered and collected the tithes, decided how and by whom they should be paid, without reference to bulls of exemption. They fixed the income of the benefices and increased or diminished them as they saw fit. They tried many ecclesiastical suits and, by the use of force, paralyzed the action of church tribunals or prelates. Lastly, no decision of the pope himself could be carried out in the Indies without permission of the king. And in the records of the early church in America are found a hundred laws or provisions emanating from the king or Council of the Indies for every bull or brief sent from Rome.*

* *Don Fray Juan de Zumarraga* (México, D.F., 1881), pp. 128-129.

Similar conditions prevailed in the Portuguese colony of Brazil. A bull issued by Pope Leo X in 1515 temporarily conferred powers of patronage upon the Portuguese crown. Then, in 1551, the Portuguese kings were denominated Permanent Grand Masters of the Order of Christ. As such, they were endowed with permanent rights of patronage.

In theory at least, the crown, whether Spanish or Portuguese, could control the secular clergy more completely than the regular clergy. Secular clergymen were directly under the control of archbishops and bishops, to whose authority they had vowed obedience. The prelates, in turn, had been nominated by and were to some degree beholden to the crown. The regulars, as members of a religious order, had taken a vow of obedience which subjected them to the discipline of a general in Rome and his subordinate representatives throughout the world. Prominent among the regular clergymen who served in the Ibero-American colonies were the Dominicans, Franciscans, Benedictines, Carmelites, Mercedarians, and Jesuits, the last of whom took, in addition to their other vows, a special one of obedience to the Pope. Concerned by the tendency of the religious orders to look to Rome rather than to Madrid for direction, King Philip II of Spain sought approval of a plan to establish a patriarchate of the Indies, centered in Madrid and endowed with virtually absolute power over all the clergy in the Spanish Indies, regular as well as secular. When the papacy denied its approval, Philip II and the able Juan de Ovando, president of the Council of the Indies, responded with the *Ordenanza del Patronazgo* of 1574. The purpose of this ordinance was to reduce the role of the regulars in the Spanish colonies and to bring about their gradual replacement by seculars. Owing in part to the scarcity of secular priests, this was never fully accomplished. The regulars continued to play an important part in the religious life of the colonies, a fact which often occasioned royal concern, particularly on the part of eighteenth-century Bourbon rulers.

While the state exercised extensive authority over the Church throughout the colonial period in Ibero-America, clergymen also enjoyed vast influence over affairs of the state. Frequently, clergymen were appointed to the highest political offices. This resulted in an overlapping of ecclesiastical and political authority. It was impossible to know where one branch of authority ended and another began. Moreover, although the Church recognized the right of royal patronage, "in fact, it aspired to override political authority each time it could, and it was accustomed to make use not only of the prestige it enjoyed with the people, but also of the influence it possessed at Court and the threats of the Inquisition." * This led inevitably to jurisdictional disputes between Church and state. As an example of such a dispute, the encounter between Archbishop Serna and Viceroy Gelves in seventeenth-century New Spain is described in one of the selections included in the first section of readings in this book.

The difficulty, given prevailing intellectual attitudes during colonial times, of distinguishing between the secular and the religious, contributed to jurisdictional disputes. The immanence of God in human society was overwhelmingly accepted as an article of faith. One need consult only a few of the early historians and chroniclers of colonial events, laymen or clerics, to become aware of the extent to which supernatural causation was ascribed to most human actions. Further, the explanations for natural phenomena were frequently sought in theological rather than in natural and scientific bodies of knowledge. Because of the manner in which God was assumed to infuse every aspect of human activity, churchmen who regarded themselves as God's servants naturally looked upon their mission as being very broad indeed. It was felt by them to extend beyond the duty of saving souls, and

---

* José Luis Romero, *A History of Argentine Political Thought*, Introduction and Translation by Thomas F. McGann (Stanford, California, 1963), p. 33.

to include the legitimate function of creating the kingdom of divine justice on earth.

The administration of temporal justice in colonial Ibero-America extended the overlapping between secular and religious interests, and consequently led to jurisdictional disputes between civil administrators and churchmen. As a special privilege or *fuero*, the Church was allowed to maintain its own system of courts. The Church insisted that all cases in which ecclesiastical discipline or the actions of churchmen were involved be tried in its own courts. Laymen, fearing they could not always expect impartial justice when dealing with ecclesiastical courts, desired to hail churchmen before civilian tribunals. Consequently, protracted debate often arose over what court enjoyed competence in a particular case.

The most important reason for chronic Church-state conflict in the Ibero-American colonies was the anticlericalism exhibited by so many of the laymen settlers. The essence of this anticlericalism was an attitude of suspiciousness and even hostility toward the administrative organization of the Church and toward most clergymen. Generally, as has remained true to the present day, Ibero-American anticlericalism did not imply willful opposition to the Roman Catholic faith. Almost subconsciously, however, something of a theological rationale was adopted to justify anticlericalism.

The Mexican historian Silvio Zavala has suggested that an unwitting tendency toward heresy inhered in the creole mentality. Without realizing that their position was in any way heretical, creoles, and for that matter their Spanish-born contemporaries as well, inclined toward the beliefs that constituted the heresy of quietism, conceived by the Spaniard Miguel de Molinos (1640-1694). One of the main tenets of quietism, as described in the *Catholic Encyclopedia* (1911) is: ". . . they who have reached perfection, i.e., complete absorption in God, have no need of external worship, or sacraments, or of prayers; they owe no obedience to any law since their will is identical with God's will."

This point of view would engender a rejection of the priestly class and the formal sacramental role of the organized Church itself. Throughout their history, Spanish—and Portuguese—American Catholics have often appeared to believe that salvation is achieved by faith alone and has no connection with the performance of actions prescribed by the positive law of the Church.

Contributing more directly toward an atmosphere of anticlericalism was the unedifying manner in which churchmen frequently quarreled among themselves: the creole and the peninsular churchmen were generally at odds, sometimes to the extent of violence. The regulars felt the seculars were too far removed from papal authority, and therefore not fit for the work of evangelization, and the various orders were consistently in conflict, as the pages of colonial history testify. In 1600, a group of seculars from Michoacán in New Spain actually invaded Nueva Galicia and put the regulars to flight. This may seem an extreme instance, but in reality such occurrences were rather commonplace. Somewhat more unusual was the action of Franciscans in sixteenth-century Chile in setting fire to an Augustinian convent.

Churchmen rarely presented a united front, and their internal bickering was bound to undermine the respect of the lay faithful. Not infrequently two different factions of churchmen maintained diametrically opposed positions, with each claiming that only its viewpoint represented the proper application of Church teachings to a particular situation. As an administrative organization concerned with practical problems, the Church was not at all a monolithic structure with a pat, party-line position in regard to the issues and problems confronting the colonists.

Another factor that nourished anticlericalism was the envy-arousing wealth of the Church. Enjoying a tax-exempt status, owning much of the finest land, controlling money-lending transactions, and with an important source of its revenue, the tithe, collected and delivered to it almost in its entirety by state officials, the Church occupied a highly privileged financial position and thus could exercise extensive temporal influence. Civilians often felt their own economic opportunities were stifled because of the unique advantages enjoyed by the Church. The Inquisition, during the seventeenth and eighteenth centuries, became a symbol to many laymen of the Church's excessive concern for and favored position in obtaining economic gain. Rumor, at this time, often had it that the Holy Office was interested less in preserving the purity of the faith than in condemning well-to-do individuals so as to confiscate their wealth.

The Inquisition in its various functions was a microcosm of the temporal and spiritual activities of the Church in colonial Latin America. The operations of the Holy Office were frequently marked by discord arising from the overlapping of ecclesiastical and civil authority, and on numerous occasions its activities led to bitter struggles among churchmen. Moreover, according to its critics, the Inquisition afforded a striking proof that the Church, which held virtually monopolistic control over education and the media of public expression, used its power to stifle curiosity, legitimate political expression, and freedom of intellectual inquiry. Referring to the consequences of the Inquisition, a nineteenth-century Argentine priest, Father Gregorio Funes of Córdoba, asserted: "In the colonial, Church-dominated period, thought was a slave and not even the soul of the citizen was his own." * Conversely, defenders of the over-all accomplishments of the Spanish colonial system tend to deny or to qualify the charge that the Inquisition suppressed intellectual freedom. The vastly differing interpretations of the operation and effects of the Inquisition are revealed in the four opening selections of the reading materials in this book. Whatever the truth may be about this conflict of opinion, it seems certain that the Inquisition was well

---

* Rómulo Carbia, *Historia de la leyenda negra hispano-americano* (Buenos Aires, 1943), p. 158.

accepted and even popular when it was first introduced in the Spanish colonies. By the end of the
colonial period, however, the Inquisition was opposed
by many and hated by some; it had become an important factor contributing to anticlericalism.

The power of the Portuguese Inquisition, established
in 1531, extended to Brazil, and the Holy Office first
proceeded against a resident of that colony in 1543.
However, no separate tribunal of the Inquisition was
ever established in Brazil. The exercise of Holy Office
powers was entrusted to bishops and other agents in
Brazil, while persons accused of offenses were sent to
Portugal for trial. Although it has been argued that
"What was lost by not having a Tribunal on the
ground was gained by the ardor with which the Familiars of the Inquisition denounced all whose acts,
words or thoughts could make them prospective cases
for the Holy Office," * still the Inquisition in Brazil
never rose to a level of importance comparable to that
of the Holy Office in Spanish America. This moderate
activity was characteristic of the general Brazilian religious scene. The Church in the huge Portuguese colony, so far as the exercise of power was concerned,
was only a dim reflection of the ecclesiastical organization in the Spanish Indies.

Nevertheless, the same sort of Church-state disputes
which often erupted in the Spanish Indies occurred
also in Brazil. Even as their Spanish counterparts did,
Brazilian churchmen struggled to gain control over
Indian affairs, justifying their actions on the grounds
of their desire to protect the aborigines against the exploitation of greedy colonists. On their part, the colonists often accused churchmen of being anxious to control Indian labor in order to enhance the temporal
wealth of the Church in general and of various religious orders in particular. A conflict over Indian policy
between Jesuits and colonists in seventeenth-century
Brazil led to virtual civil war, and one phase of the

---

* Bailey W. Diffie, *Latin American Civilization: Colonial
Period* (Harrisburg, Pa., 1945), p. 737.

clash is described in the selection that concludes the first section of readings.

The rise of the independence movement in Hispanic America presented the Church with new difficulties, revealing that the clergy was more than ever divided among its own members, and just as inclined as always to regard political questions in a theological light. While some churchmen in Mexico prayed to the *Virgin de los Remedios* to hasten the success of the divinely-favored royalist cause, others invoked the intercession of the *Virgin de Guadalupe* to speed the providentially-preferred patriot victory.

The overwhelming majority of the hierarchy, which was born in Spain and which felt that the Church could not maintain its exalted position if deprived of the support of the Spanish crown, tended to regard favorable attitudes toward independence as impious if not downright heretical. A large number of native-born Spanish-American clergy, on the other hand, including both creoles and mestizos, favored independence and worked zealously to attain it. Fathers Miguel Hidalgo and José María Morelos, prominent among the early leaders of Mexico's struggle against Spain, Luis Beltrán, the great metallurgist and munitions maker in La Plata and Chile, and Camilio Henríquez, founder of Chile's first newspaper, were a few among the many leaders whom the clergy contributed to the patriot cause.

So far as the future position of the Hispanic-American Church was concerned, the period of the revolutionary wars was a particularly poor time for the clergy to divide, even more uncompromisingly than usual, among themselves. Independence, as an accomplished fact, was soon to present the Church with the greatest temporal challenge it had confronted in Hispanic America. During the colonial period, in spite of not infrequent clashes between representatives of royal and clerical interests, the crown consistently prevented civilian forces from striking genuinely crippling blows against the Church. On its part, the Church generally impressed upon the masses their duty to respect royal authority. At times, Inquisition officials seemed as concerned about stamping out signs of treason as extirpating heresy. There was a symbolic relationship between Church and state which worked to the advantage of both.

With the coming of independence to Spanish America, Church-state relations underwent a dramatic transformation. Gone was the crown, the great political institution and the one power that had been able to control contending administrative agencies. The Church remained. But without the backing of the crown, its position as an unassailable bastion of privilege was in jeopardy. Accordingly, the Church entered more directly into the political arena, hoping through political action to protect its customary rights and privileges. As often as not, the Church sustained defeat in its political ventures. When this occurred, civilian groups, at last able to give meaningful expression to their long pent-up hostility toward churchmen, moved quickly to strip the Church of its temporal power. Sometimes they even took advantage of the Church's political discomfiture to deprive it of the effective means to exercise its spiritual office. They proceeded to this extreme not only because of intellectual conviction, but because of the desire to stamp out any vestige of influence that the Church could conceivably find useful in staging a political comeback.

Even while Latin American revolutions for independence from Spain were still in progress, heated dispute between Church and state officials had burst forth over the issue of patronage. The insurrectionary governments claimed that they had inherited the patronage rights once exercised by the Spanish crown. Patronage, they insisted, was one of the inalienable prerogatives of sovereignty. Therefore, when new groups acquired sovereign control over areas once ruled by Spain, they gained the rights of patronage that had inhered in the Spanish crown. On the other hand, many churchmen contended that control over patronage had been bestowed upon the monarchs as a special, temporary, and revokable privilege. The loss of sovereignty by the crown, they asserted, meant that the Church should reclaim authority over religious affairs and so begin to exercise directly the powers of patronage.

Independence had scarcely been won when political leaders and churchmen began to argue over taxation. Should, for example, the national government continue the colonial tradition of collecting tithes for the Church? Invariably, this question precipitated serious disagreements. The separate Church courts, provided for by the ecclesiastical *fuero* of colonial times, also came in for attack. Gradually, they were abolished by national administrations. Much Church property was also seized and a substantial number of religious communities were suppressed, occasionally against a background of violence.

The issues of patronage, Church taxes, separate ecclesiastical courts, and Church property had already been fought out to a large degree in various European nations, beginning as early as the eleventh century, and by 1800 had been substantially resolved. Although in the process the temporal power of the Church had been weakened, in general its rights to minister to the spiritual needs of its followers had not been denied. In Latin America, vexatious problems that had concerned Europeans for centuries were resolved in the course of a few short years.

Other disputes which had erupted generations and even centuries previously in Europe, and for which certain accommodations had been arranged, appeared in Latin America only after the attainment of independence. For a variety of reasons, many political leaders in the new republics sought to limit Church control over education and charity. In several Latin American countries cemeteries were secularized so as to deprive the Church of the formidable power to deny burial in the *campo santo* (consecrated ground) to those who had incurred its displeasure. Laws were also passed to remove marriage from the control of the Church by providing for the legality, sometimes the exclusive legality, of civil marriage contracts. In addition, some republics enacted laws of religious toleration during the nineteenth century. To these measures Church authorities often replied with massive excommunications. At other times, supported by large numbers of the lay faithful, they resorted to civil insurrection.

During this period Latin Americans did not develop indigenous intellectual movements, but looked to Europe for philosophical guidance. The anticlerical aspect of nineteenth-century European liberalism found fertile ground in an environment where hostility toward the clergy had long existed. Furthermore, particularly in Mexico, Chile, and Brazil, intellectuals were influenced by the positivism of Auguste Comte. Positivism proclaimed that the laws of progress for civilizations could be discovered only by scientific, empirical investigation. Positivists equated revealed truth with superstition and maintained that formal religions must be swept away so that allegedly obscurantist, unfounded views could not stand in the way of progress based upon scientific truth.

The changes in status with which the Church was threatened during this period meant an inevitable reduction of its material and temporal strength. Churchmen, however, tended to interpret any attempt to alter the *status quo* as inimical to religion itself. They were largely justified in this alarmist viewpoint, precisely because most champions of change and reform believed that the Church, *per se*, was incompatible with modern progress. Clerical fear of novelty sprang also from the manner in which many churchmen of the previous century had indiscriminately welcomed the ideas of the Enlightenment. This movement had led to notable scientific and economic progress in Latin America, as well as to a remarkable freedom of intellectual activity. However, in Latin America the Enlightenment in its ultimate effects also spawned a lack of respect for authority, a religious relativism, and a secularism which redounded to the serious disadvantage of the Church and the values it defended. Because they had once been beguiled by what had appeared to be ideas that were useful and yet not opposed to formal religion, churchmen became hyper-cautious and consistently opposed manifestations of the new.

Church authorities and their lay partisans in the late nineteenth century insisted that the only unifying, constructive tradition from which Latin Americans could establish order and achieve progress was the Catholic tradition of colonial times. To depart from it, they contended, would produce chaos and political institutions that were distorted and unnatural because they were not rooted in the past. Diego Portales of Chile (the dominant political figure from 1830 to 1837), Gabriel García Moreno of Ecuador (sometimes the president and always the main political power from 1860 to 1875), and Rafael Núñez of Colombia (the president or president-maker from 1880 to 1894) were among those controversial statesmen who felt it necessary to preserve the traditional power and influence of the Church as a means of attaining national unity and stability. Similar viewpoints have been championed by many Latin American intellectuals down to the present time, and are reflected in the selection from the writings of Aurelio Espinosa Polit. On the other hand, anticlerical leaders insisted that the Catholic tradition was one of sterility and oppression. Their viewpoint is succinctly described in the selection by William Rex Crawford. It is manifested also, in extreme form, by a statement of the nineteenth-century Chilean journalist Domingo Arteaga Alemparte: "So deplorable has been the record of the Church in regard to political interference that it is impossible for a Catholic to be a good citizen." *

The struggle between liberal, anticlerical forces and conservative, proclerical groups was violent and pro-

---

* See Pedro N. Cruz, *Estudios sobre literatura chilena* (Santiago de Chile, 1926), I, p. 3.

tracted in Guatemala, Ecuador and Colombia. The passion with which Colombians of these two respective camps assailed each other during the nineteenth century is reflected in the works of many national historians. Writing in 1938, Colombia's liberal author Jorge Espinosa Londoño referred to the origins of the Church-state dispute in the national period:

The fanaticism of the population was the polar star for the leaders of the reactionary movement. . . . In waging their political fights, the Conservatives always associated their cause with that of the Divinity. Ultimately, they profaned the name of Christ. . . . Those people taking up the banner of religion confused, or found it expedient to seem to confuse, the purely political actions of the government with the universal principles of religion.*

José Manuel Groot, a conservative intellectual of the past century, interprets events from an opposite point of view:

Peace and harmony could have been established then [in 1830], but the uncurbed passions of the anticlerical, liberal forces did not permit this, and the unhappy consequences have continued to plague the country, bringing discord, combat, and revolution. . . . The truth is that the ecclesiastical and political life of our nation had been always so intertwined that religion was necessarily the vital element of all our civilization and progress.†

It was in Mexico that the struggle between Church and state reached a peak of bitterness, doing much to shape the character of Mexican history throughout the national period. The intensity of partisan emotions which this dispute evoked is suggested by the statements of two Mexican historians. The liberal Alfonso Toro declares:

The clergy had made of colonial society an assembly of hypocritical and subservient human beings. The priests

---

* *Pascual Bravo: los partidos políticos en Colombia* (Medellín, 1938), pp. 53, 251.
† *Historia eclesiástica y civil de Nueva Granada* (Bogotá, 1953 edition), V, p. 515 and I, p. 7.

made the Mexicans as ignorant as they were, as dirty,
immoral and lazy as they were. Accordingly, the reformers
have always tended to root out these vices, seeking to
reduce the clergy to its proper role and to deprive it of
the property it has collected and monopolized to the
disadvantage of the people.*

At the opposite extreme Félix Navarrete maintains:

The detractors of the Church pretend that grounds have
existed for a struggle between the Church and the civil
power since the earliest period of the discovery of Mexico,
and that this fight has always been provoked by the
Church. I say that grounds for this struggle have existed
in Mexico only since 1833, the year in which Masonry
provoked it so as to bring an end to the influence of the
clergy and even to the clergy itself. From that time on the
Church has only defended itself against attacks.†

Because of the seriousness of the dispute between
Church and state in Mexico, two fairly substantial selections, included in the reading material about Latin
America's first century of independence, relate to that
country. Although written in the 1930's, these selections are characterized by impassioned, emotional dis-
agreement over the interpretation of events that transpired between 1854 and 1876. That the conflict between Church and state can be discussed in a calm,
detached, and scholarly manner rather than in terms
of the struggle between good and evil is revealed by the
Francis M. Stanger article describing the issue in Peru,
and above all by the excerpt from the writings of J.
Lloyd Mecham, summarizing the results of the clericalism vs. anticlericalism rivalry of the first century of the
national period.

Brazil, because it remained a monarchy for sixty-
seven years after declaring its independence from
Portugal, maintained intact many aspects of the ad-

---

* *La iglesia y el estado en México: estudio sobre los conflictos
entre el clero católico y los gobiernos mexicanos desde la independencia hasta nuestros días* (México, D.F., 1927), p. 43.
† *La lucha entre el poder civil y el clero a la luz de la historia*
(El Paso, Texas, 1935), p. 230.

ministrative institutions fashioned during the colonial period. The relationship between Church and state was not altered essentially, and the battles that marked the dealings of churchmen with political leaders in the Spanish-American republics were largely absent from Brazilian development. In part, this was because Brazilian Catholicism had developed a greater flexibility and spirit of compromise than Hispanic-American Catholicism. It is notable that in 1810 a Portuguese-English treaty extended rights to the British to build a Protestant church in Rio de Janeiro, although it had to look like a private house and could not use bells to summon worshippers. The Bishop of Rio, José Caetano, strongly favored this concession to Protestant believers. It is difficult to imagine a similar response from a Spanish prelate in the year 1810.

The remarkable figure of Fr. Diogo Antônio Feijó also imparted an unusual character to Church-state relations in the early years of Brazilian independence. Fr. Feijó, regent of Brazil from 1835 to 1837, was a pious priest and at the same time the leader of anti-clerical forces who demanded the superiority of civil over ecclesiastical authority, and the confiscation of the wealth of the religious orders. Moreover, Fr. Feijó abandoned the wearing of his clerical garb and led an unsuccessful campaign for legislation to permit the clergy to marry.

The most dramatic and consequential Church-state clash in nineteenth-century Brazil erupted in 1872, and involved the attempt of two bishops to promulgate and enforce instructions from the Vatican that had not been officially cleared by civil authorities. Although the dispute left unpleasant memories on both sides, it did not generate the sort of bitterness that prevailed in several of Brazil's sister republics of Latin America. When the monarchy was overthrown and Brazil became a republic in 1889, Church and state officials were able within a short time to reach an amicable agreement upon separation of the two powers.

The liberal movements in nineteenth-century Latin

America had, in many instances, been led by members of the aristocracy. When the liberal cause triumphed, little if any social upheaval occurred. Around the turn of the century, however, new middle groups began to emerge in the more advanced countries of Latin America. In the overwhelming majority of instances, these new groups were comprised of urban elements, depending for livelihood on commerce, manufacturing, or other business operations of a non-agrarian nature. Basically, the clergymen tended to be suspicious of, if not actually hostile to, the emerging middle class. They feared that the alleged materialism of the new capitalist class would threaten the supremacy of the spiritual values upon which the Church insisted. Traditionally, moreover, the Church in Latin America had prospered best when allied with the owners of the huge landed estates. Its ability to retain temporal power, or to re-acquire it in those countries where it had been diminished or totally suppressed, seemed to depend upon the continuing strength of the landed aristocracy, and upon the preservation of a semi-feudal social structure in which neither the masters nor the serfs would oppose a privileged position for the Church. The rise to power of a new urban group, over which the Church had virtually no control, threatened the supremacy of an established order in which the Church was strongly entrenched.

In spite of hostile Church attitudes, new middle groups began to acquire political power in the more advanced Latin American republics at different periods in the twentieth century. Throughout the area their strength is growing, and in some republics they exercise the dominant political power. The men who make up these new groups have realized that in general the clergy has viewed them with hostile eyes. They have, therefore, been predisposed to continue and sometimes to intensify the struggle against the Church initiated in the previous century.

Although events in the nineteenth and twentieth centuries altered the traditional pattern of relations between Church and state in most Latin American countries, traditionalism remained largely unchallenged in regard to one important aspect of the social structure. While new middle groups were achieving positions of social, economic, and political importance, almost nothing was accomplished toward incorporating the vast lower mass into society. This fact constitutes the principal source of existing and potential political conflict involving the Church in contemporary Latin America.

The lower mass in Latin America is no longer docile, patient, and fatalistically resigned to a life of perpetual poverty. Crowding into the cities in a remarkable demographic shift that has seen the percentage of rural inhabitants decline rapidly, millions of former peasants have swelled the ranks of the urban proletariat. Able now to view the opportunities for material advance that life in the modern city can bring to those who are actual participants in society, they have become discontented with their role as nonparticipants in the economic and political life of their nations. The nature of future developments in Latin America depends to a great extent upon the type of leadership that the masses receive in their effort to join in the life of the twentieth century.

During recent generations churchmen have had little direct contact with the masses. In many Latin American countries the poverty of the Church and the scarcity of priests would have made this contact difficult to achieve, even when the desire for it existed. A contributing factor to this situation was the fact that the religious life of the lower classes seemed to present no immediate practical problem to the Church. Although most generally not practicing Catholics, and although usually startlingly ignorant about the faith, the great majority of the masses had at least an overwhelming predisposition toward Catholicism. More important, they had no alternative to being half-formed Catholics.

Today the masses have an alternative. Those who

have flocked into the cities can join the Protestant churches that have been established in Latin America in mounting number. They can also join overtly antireligious movements, and they can become communists. Moreover, the role of Indian peasants in demanding radical land reform in Bolivia in 1953, the massive unrest among the northeastern Brazilian peasants and their support of the leftist Francisco Julião, and developments in Cuba since the inception of Fidel Castro's Sierra Maestra campaign in December, 1956, reveal the potentially favorable disposition of the rural masses toward Marxian expedients.

In the mid-twentieth century, then, the Church has had to concern itself with the masses. More and more its prelates have begun to speak out in favor of social justice. However, as has been true so often in the past, the Church is divided. Social justice has divergent meanings to different churchmen. To one group it means preserving the stratified, closed society. Men of this persuasion believe that if charitable work is expanded and paternalistic measures are more conscientiously applied, the masses will once again become content to remain in their place and will abandon any thought of challenging their superiors. The material by Jorge Iván Hübner included here demonstrates this approach to the social problem. The views of Hübner are in accord with those of many conservative Catholics throughout Latin America. On the other hand, numerous Catholics contend that the old social structure is doomed and that paternalism and charity will never suffice to keep the masses in line. They envision the emergence of genuine social pluralism in which all classes and functional interest groups will have the power to protect their essential rights and to compete on a basis of relative equality of opportunity for the advantages the nation has to offer. Latin America's Christian Democratic movement, especially in Chile where it has attained its greatest strength, urges this approach to the social problem. This fact is clearly revealed in the excerpts from two of the books of

Eduardo Frei, for many years the leading figure in Chile's Christian Democratic Party.

How has the new interest of churchmen and of the Catholic laity in the social problem renewed the Church-state conflict? Whatever their differences of opinion as to what constitutes the ideal social system, churchmen and the practicing Catholic laity are convinced that a just social order can exist only if it is based upon the moral teachings of the Church. Therefore, they firmly believe that the Church must speak out boldly on the social problem, propose solutions, and insist upon the attempt to apply these solutions. This belief is expressed in the writing reproduced in this book of the archbishop of Guatemala. Conflict arises because the supporters of most twentieth-century reform moves that have come to power in Latin America or aspire to attain it are anticlerical and secular in orientation. Such men, whose anticlericalism is often attributable to the fact that they come from the new middle sectors once resolutely opposed by clergymen, are not disposed to allow the Church a role in helping to formulate social change.

The issue of whether or not the Church should share in devising and implementing social reform programs helped lead to the sharp conflict between ecclesiastical leaders and Juan Perón in Argentina. This conflict, as viewed from the anticlerical position, is described in the excerpt from the Perón speech and from an editorial of an official Peronist journal which are included in this book. As a result of the Argentine dispute, a bishop and a canon of the Buenos Aires Cathedral were exiled, the president of the republic was excommunicated, and several churches were burned.

The social justice issue has contributed to renewed political controversy involving religious questions in Mexico. The official party and the dominant political force in that country is the anticlerical Revolutionary Institutional Party (*Partido Revolucionario Institucional*), or the PRI, as it is called by Mexicans. The PRI has begun to express resentment over the criticism of the opposition Party of National Action (*Partido de Acción Nacional*), known as the PAN. The excerpt included from a 1960 publication of its youth organization shows that the PAN has been upbraiding the PRI for its alleged inattentiveness to social reform and for allowing large-scale communist infiltration. PAN members, who are beginning to refer to themselves as Christian Democrats, also argue that only the implementation of Catholic principles can lead to a just social order. The concluding selection in this book, an excerpt from a book by Robert E. Scott, suggests that the official Mexican Party, the PRI, has made steady political, economic, and social progress. The implication is that there may be little need for the type of improvement, purportedly Christian in nature, which the PAN insists only it can introduce.

Elsewhere in Latin America, signs of Church-state tension have begun once more to appear. The separation of Church and state in Chile, effected in 1925, has produced generally harmonious relations between the two powers. In September of 1962, however, the Chilean ecclesiastical hierarchy issued a pastoral letter lamenting the social injustices that were said to be glaringly evident throughout the country.* The hierarchy further contended that a capitalistic system based upon the classically liberal concepts of unfettered economic individualism could not produce a just society. Almost at once Chile's Liberal Party, one of the country's most powerful political groups, began to issue indignant denunciations of the Church's alleged interference in political matters.

Centering in Chile, Colombia, Venezuela and Costa Rica, but existing also more weakly throughout the Latin American republics, is a movement aimed at the organization of Christian trade unions which base their programs largely on the social teachings of the Catholic Church. To coordinate the efforts of these national associations, the Latin American Confederation of

---

* *Los Obispos de Chile Hablan: el deber social y político en la hora presenta* (Santiago de Chile, 1962).

Trade Unionists (referred to generally by its Spanish initials, CLASC) has been established, together with a rural branch known as the Latin American Federation of Farm Laborers (FLAC). Early in 1963, after completing a tour of Latin America, Auguste Vanistendael, secretary general of the International Federation of Christian Trade Unions, stated: "Christian trade unions will be the dominant social-political groups in Latin America within a few years." * This statement may exaggerate the influence that the Christian trade union movement is likely to have, for it is opposed even by many practicing Catholics who are scrupulously intent upon avoiding what might be even remotely construed as the interjection of the religious issue into areas considered by many to be purely political. Still, those who exercise governing power south of the Rio Grande, who are often accustomed to having tight control over labor organizations, can be expected to distrust and even to be hostile toward any new labor movement which looks to the social doctrines of the Catholic Church for inspiration rather than to national political programs.

The issue of Church and state and the social problem is complicated still further by the presence of Catholic reform advocates who regard the way of Christian Democracy as being too mild and traditionalist. In northeastern Brazil, for example, Father Antônio Melo Costa leads the Catholic Peasant Movement, which has come to include more than forty separate unions. He approves some of the objectives of Communism and "Fidelism," regarding them as compatible with Christianity, and has expressed certain doubts that adequate social reforms can be achieved through traditional processes of so-called democracy as they presently operate in Brazil. Should government officials decide that Fr. Melo Costa is becoming too troublesome a critic of their policies, Church authorities might have difficulty in deciding whether to support the zealous clerical reformer or the state.

---

* *Ave Maria*, Vol. 97 (January 19, 1963), 4.

As the social problem in Latin America becomes increasingly acute, a new variant in the conflict between Church and state could become a major issue—especially if the power of Marxism continues to mount among influential groups. The future status of Church-state relations will depend largely upon the ability of churchmen and middle-class political leaders, just those groups which in the past have frequently demonstrated mutual antagonism, to find a basis for cooperation in responding to Latin America's social crisis.

In what must be taken as a criticism of the past record of middle-sector political groups, Stanford University's John J. Johnson has expressed the hope that the rising influence of Christian democracy "could provide a moral fiber in political life that the political parties themselves have not produced." * The majority of Latin America's politicians might not agree that they lack a moral fiber which could be provided by Christian democracy. On the other hand, how many of the southern continent's Church leaders would agree with the statement made by the University of Notre Dame's John J. Kennedy at a 1962 conference on "Explosive Forces in Latin America."

Too often churchmen seem to be the prisoners of their own statistics. The national census reports that about ninety-eight per cent of the population is Catholic; in reality, only twenty to thirty per cent may be active Church members. . . . Open acknowledgement of the fact that not all Latin Americans are practicing Catholics could, however, be an important first step in creating an atmosphere where the Church's legitimate interest in social reform could be exercised in conjunction with other reform interests with a minimum of conflict.†

---

* *Political Changes in Latin America: The Emergence of the Middle Sectors* (Stanford, California, 1958), p. 69.

† This conference was held November 1-3, under the auspices of the Graduate Institute for World Affairs, the Ohio State University, and of the Mershon Center on Education in National Defense. The papers have been published in John J. TePaske and Sydney Nettleton Fisher, eds., *Explosive Forces in Latin America* (Columbus: Ohio State University Press, 1964). The Kennedy quotation is on p. 53.

The conflict between Church and state is too deeply imbedded in the historical tradition of Latin America to disappear altogether within the foreseeable future. Along with such controversial matters as the role of the military, the value of democracy, and the applicability of Marxian economic analysis in newly emerging republics, it will continue to be a consequential issue. If not the principal theme in the future of Latin American development, it is likely to remain a distinctly audible obbligato accompaniment to that theme. To students in the United States, the heirs of a historical tradition that differs vastly from that of Latin America, the Church-state issue South of the Border will not cease to be a source of perplexity and puzzlement—until its centuries-old evolutionary process is painstakingly analyzed.

• I •

THE

Colonial Period

JOSÉ TORIBIO MEDINA

The Tribunal of the Holy Office of the Inquisition in Colonial Spanish America

Seeking documents pertaining to the colonial history of his native Chile, José Toribio Medina proceeded to Spain in 1884. In the town of Simancas he discovered, in a damp, subterranean vault known as the Cubicle of the Bishop, a massive amount of material dealing with the Inquisition in the Spanish American colonies. An indefatigable researcher and a dedicated bibliophile, Medina set himself to the study of these documents, soon realizing that the information they contained would necessitate the revision of many aspects of traditional Spanish American colonial history. Between 1887 and 1914 Medina published nine volumes on the Inquisition in the Spanish Indies. No Latin American writer has engaged in more extensive research on the activities of the Holy Office in the Spanish colonies.

THE arrogance and the insolence of the Inquisitors, which from the very beginning knew no limits, was fostered by the impunity to all ordinary legal processes and restrictions which applied not only to them but to all of their relatives. It is utterly impossible to relate the innumerable quarrels, difficulties, and unpleasant-

From José Toribio Medina, *Historia del Tribunal del Santo Oficio de la Inquisición en Chile* (Santiago de Chile, 1952 ed.), excerpts from pp. 109-131. By permission of the Fondo Histórico y Bibliográfico José Toribio Medina, Santiago de Chile.

ries of all kinds with which Inquisitors harassed civil authorities, beginning with the viceroys, and even other churchmen during the two and a half centuries that the Holy Office functioned in the Spanish domains of America. The fact that the king had bestowed vast powers upon them might have been endurable if the ministers of the Tribunal had been content to exercise their authority within the confines originally intended. Only three years after the establishment of the Inquisition, however, the *audiencia* of Lima had already begun to send its denunciations of inquisitorial abuse to the monarch. Complaints and denunciations against the Inquisition continued in an unending chain, often being lodged by the very archbishops of Lima.

In view of the innumerable denunciations which were being received, one may say on a daily basis, the crown felt obliged to take measures to stop—so far as possible—the abuses of which the ministers of the Inquisition were guilty. Accordingly, the Spanish king determined that two members of the General Council and two of the Council of the Indies should meet to devise a set of regulations that would govern the conduct of the Inquisitors and would clearly stipulate the nature of the relations they were to have with civil authorities. The regulations were duly formulated and approved by a royal decree of 1610. This decree has always been known as the *Concordia*. In truth, the *Concordia* contained in each of its twenty-six articles sentences which condemned the actions of the ministers of the Tribunal of Lima.

For example, it was ordered that henceforth the Inquisitors must not directly or indirectly, either themselves or through third persons, interfere on their own behalf or in behalf of friends and relatives, in the renting of royal possessions. Inquisitors were also ordered to cease commercial operations, either carried on directly or through the instrumentality of a third person. They were further forbidden to take merchandise against the will of the owner, and were ordered not to forbid the sailing of any ship or the departure of any person from the ports of Peru simply because a ship or a person did not have a permit from the Inquisition. The Tribune's ministers were cautioned to appoint as familiars [*familiares*], or subordinate officials, people of quiet life and honest habits. They were further instructed not to afford protection to Inquisition officials who also held civil office and who while exercising this office were guilty of wrongdoing of any kind, including living in concubinage. Finally, Inquisitors were ordered not to institute proceedings of censure against viceroys when competition arose between the Holy Office and the viceroy over jurisdiction in a particular case.

The insolence and pride of the Inquisitors should not surprise us. They were, after all, protected by the supreme authority of the pope and the king. During these times, no greater authority after God was recognized on the face of the earth.

Whenever the Inquisition performed in public any of the ceremonies related to the fulfillment of its functions, it was very careful to demand that the viceroy attend and subscribe to the following oath that was read by an Inquisitor:

Your Eminence swears and promises by his faith and word that as a true Catholic viceroy in the service of His Catholic Majesty he will defend with all his power the Catholic Faith that Our Holy Mother the Apostolic Church of Rome holds and believes; that he will maintain and expand it; that he will persecute and have persecuted heretics and apostates; that he will assist with all necessary means the Holy Office of the Inquisition and its ministers so that heretics who disturb our Christian religion may be jailed and punished according to the tenets of Canon Law, without any fault on his part and without any exception in favor of any person, regardless of his condition.

The viceroy then replied, "Thus do I swear and promise by my faith and word." Following this the same Inquisitor continued: "Acting in this way, as we expect you to do because of your religious fervor and Christian faith, you and all of the actions which you perform in the holy service of Our Lord will be exalted. He will give you long life and the good health which your services in this kingdom require."

Because of the tremendous powers enjoyed by the Tribunal, there was actually a period in which no one could depart from Peruvian ports without the special permit of the Holy Office. Its ministers were also present at the arrival of every ship to investigate the very words that had been spoken during the voyage. It was impossible to print even a line without the Inquisition's approval. Prelates, *audiencia* justices, and royal officials had to collect and destroy—according to royal laws—all forbidden books, and in general all books brought by foreigners who came to the Indies.

Given the situation as described, it is easy to understand that it was impossible to live in security or to trust anyone, even the members of one's own family. It happened many times that the husband denounced his wife, the wife her husband, the brother his brother, the friar his fellow friars, and so on. The ears of the Tribunal were always open to the most absurd accusations as well as to denunciations inspired by revenge, envy, and jealousy. Not even the penitent who sought the repose of his soul in the confessional at the feet of a priest was safe from the Inquisition. As the Augustinian Calancha has accurately said, all religious were the spies and sentries of the Inquisition, and all the faithful were its servants.

While the Tribunal became hateful to many, no men had better reason to detest it than the miserable creatures who had been placed in its secret jails. To begin with, they had to make long journeys, usually chained, just because of a simple accusation quite often made by only one witness, perhaps an enemy. Viceroys frequently complained about the rigors of these journeys. Once arrived at the prison, the suspects were given insufficient food. Tortures were inflicted upon them to make them confess imaginary crimes. They were subjected to the most outrageous personal indignities and all the while, during the never-ending process, they were denied the right to know the identity of their accusers. All of this constituted such an Odyssey of suffering for the miserably afflicted unfortunates that frequently they sought an end to their sufferings through painful suicides, bleeding themselves to death, hanging themselves, denying themselves food, and even trying to suffocate themselves—which seems unbelievable—by stuffing rags into their mouths. What perhaps seems even more horrible to our modern societies is that the Tribunal vented its rage not only upon these unfortunate victims, but upon their children who were frequently left orphans. These children were deprived of the goods that belonged to them as the inheritance of their fathers, and were even condemned to live in perpetual infamy—sharing with their parents the shame for crimes never committed.

From our point of view, the most interesting aspect of the sentences imposed by the Inquisition lies in the contrast between punishments meted out on one hand to those who had sinned against the faith, and on the other to those who had violated the norms of accepted custom. Thus, Francisco Moyen who denied that sins against the Sixth Commandment constituted punishable actions was sentenced to thirteen years in prison plus ten years in exile. Vastly different was the fate of a priest who in the confessional abused his female penitents to the fullest extent possible. His punishment consisted only of a more-or-less short suspension of his powers to hear confession and of a few spiritual penances. This repulsive contrast is indeed surprising.

Notwithstanding all of this, it is undeniable that the Holy Office, whose name ultimately invoked fear in every person, was generally applauded when founded in America. "The Holy Tribunal of the Inquisition," said the well-known Calancha a little more than fifty years after its establishment in the City of the Kings, "is a tree planted by God so that each of its branches extending over Christendom could be the staff of justice with flowers of mercy and fruits of punishment." Exactly a century after this passage was printed another writer, as well-known and respected in Lima as the one just quoted, Doctor Pedro Peralta Barnuevo, declared:

The Inquisition is a sun in which has been brought together all the rays of light previously scattered about the globe of religion. This Holy Tribunal is the fortress of faith and the watchtower of its purity. It is the tabernacle that guards the Ark; it is the fence that defends the vineyard of God and the tower from which it is possible to discover who is likely to attack; it is the shepherd who protects the Catholic flock against the wolf of error, against the impious and the heretical who seek to take away from God His faithful. It is the river of the Celestial Jerusalem that flows from the throne of the Lamb, irrigating with the waters of its refulgent purity the tree of the religion whose leaves are the salvation of Christianity. Its sacred ministers are the swift angels sent to help protect the people against the seducers who try to tear them asunder and to sow discord among them.

From the outset, however, it was obvious that the bishops generally did not receive with pleasure the establishment of the Inquisition within their respective dioceses. Perhaps this was because a great deal of their jurisdiction was thereby removed from them. Also, as time went by, they discovered that the ministers of the Inquisition were constant critics of their conduct, if not gratuitous slanderers. In this respect, the Inquisition was utterly without scruple. The prelates who in fulfillment of their duties thought it their obligation to formulate even the slightest remonstrance in regard to inquisitorial practices were denounced and quite often pitilessly slandered. This was a technique that from the very beginning the Inquisitors mastered and one to which they invariably resorted.

Merriment and gayety greeted the news of the abolition of the Tribunal in Lima. Accompanying the news also were many manifestations of hatred on the part of the people against the Holy Office. It is clear, then, that the passage of time did not serve to preserve the favorable opinion of the Inquisition that had been widespread at the time of its inception.

Divided among themselves and so hostile to each other that they lived in perpetual hatred of one another; insolent with everyone, even with their own familiars; revengeful to the point of never forgiving anyone who dared to denounce them or even to talk badly about them; constantly searching in their archives to find traces of the most concealed incriminating secrets of those whom they had decided to persecute, and fabricating evidence when they could not discover it; fulfilling their functions so carelessly that it is very difficult to find even one case prosecuted according to their own laws—as the documents of the proceedings testify; beginning by making themselves hateful and horrible to everyone and ending by being held in mockery and derision without a vestige of prestige; supported invariably by people of their own sort, men who were animated by revenge and avarice and who led their lives in ignorance and dissipation; cruel to an unbelievable degree, and finally dying as they had lived: such were the ministers who under the name of the Holy Office were in charge of defending the faith and maintaining its purity in the Spanish domains of South America.

HENRY CHARLES LEA

The Inquisition in Colonial Peru

Henry Charles Lea was born in Philadelphia in 1825
and died in the same city in 1909. He published more
than twelve carefully researched books, dealing mainly
with the late medieval Catholic Church and in particular with the Inquisition. Suffering from chronic poor
health yet serving as the head of an important Philadelphia publishing house, Lea did his research and most of
his writing at night.

His study of the Inquisition in Spain is still a vitally
important reference source, although numerous critics
have written on its alleged shortcomings and prejudiced
interpretations. Lea, whose early spiritual guidance
came primarily from his Quaker father, believed that
no historical writing was worthwhile unless it conveyed
a moral. The moral he wished to impart to the readers
of his work on the Inquisition in the Spanish colonies
was that the Holy Office, by preventing orderly and
systematic administration, by encouraging strife and
controversy, had hastened Spain's loss of its depend-
encies and had virtually prevented the newly independent republics from achieving adequate political
and economic development.

WHEN, on January 9, 1570, Serván de Cerezuela arrived at Lima to open a Tribunal of the Inquisition,
the condition of Spanish South America was such as
to call for energetic action if the colony was to respond
to the hopes of those who had so earnestly urged the

Christianization of the New World. The establishment there of the Holy Office had been asked for by many who viewed with dismay the prevailing demoralization, and we shall see whether its influence proved to be for good or for evil. Peru had been conquered by adventurers inflamed with the thirst of gold, who in the eager search for wealth had thrown off the restraints of civilized life. The Church exercised little or no moral power for, as the existing Viceroy, Francisco de Toledo, reported, he found on his arrival that the clerics and *frailes* [members of religious orders],* bishops and prelates, were lords of the spiritual and acknowledged no superior in the temporal. The king was exposed to constant outlays in granting free passage by every fleet to great numbers of clerics and frailes who came under the pretext of converting and teaching the Indians, but, in reality, many devoted themselves to accumulating wealth, plucking the Indians in the endeavor to return to Spain with fortunes. These priests kept prisons, *alguaciles* [constables] and chains, seizing and punishing all who offended them and there was no one to call them to account.

As regards matters of faith, in the absence of the Inquisition, the jurisdiction over heresy, inherent in the episcopal office, had reasserted itself and was exercised by the bishops. The bishops did not willingly acquiesce in the surrender of a jurisdiction which could be so profitably employed. That Archbishop Loaiza showed a recalcitrant temper is manifested by a letter of the *Suprema* [the supreme governing body of the Inquisition with its headquarters in Spain] directing that he should not style himself *"inquisitor ordinario"* in his pastorals and edicts. Another letter permits him to inspect the commissions of the inquisitors and their instructions if he desires, but it must be in the audience-chamber as they are not to be removed from there, except the printed instructions, of which a copy may be given to him on condition of his allowing no one

---

* All bracketed material has been added by the editor.

to see it. There was evident friction despite the injunctions of the Suprema that a good understanding should be maintained. This was increased when, in 1574, a royal *cédula* addressed to the bishops ordered them to exercise special vigilance and make secret inquiry about disguised Lutheran preachers who were said to be on their way to Peru. The prelates assumed this to be a grant of renewed inquisitorial power and undertook to exercise it, giving rise to no little trouble. Sebastián de Lartaún, bishop of Cuzco, not only published edicts trespassing on inquisitorial jurisdiction but boasted that, if the inquisitors came into his diocese, he could punish them, and he arrested and imprisoned in chains their commissioner Pedro de Quiroga, a canon of his cathedral, publicly and under circumstances of great scandal. The Tribunal retaliated by summoning to Lima the bishop's provisor Albornoz and throwing him in the secret prison; furthermore it imprisoned the priest Luis de Arma, who had assisted in chaining Quiroga, as well as the episcopal fiscal Alonso Durán and a cleric named Bejerano for the same offence, to which the bishop responded by seizing Quiroga's temporalities and forbidding him to enter the church. The tribunal, in 1581, reported the situation to the Suprema, which replied that nothing was to be conceded to the Ordinaries save what was allowed by the laws and the royal cédulas.

Thus early commenced the antagonism between the Inquisition and the episcopate which continued during its whole career to be a disturbing element in the Spanish possessions. In 1584 we find Inquisitor Ulloa complaining to the Suprema of the action of the recent provincial council of Lima in secretly writing to the king about the evil character of the commissioners selected. This, he asserts, arose from his refusal of the request of the bishops of Cuzco, La Plata and Tucumán to make them commissioners in their respective dioceses. The bishops, he adds, were opposed to the introduction of the Inquisition, because it limited their jurisdiction, and they and the royal courts were con-

stantly causing trouble in spite of the extreme modesty
and deference shown by his officials.

We have seen that Cerezuela was alone in opening
the Tribunal. The fiscal, Alcedo, and the notary,
Arrieta, were quarrelling mortally with each other, and
both were writing to the Suprema criticizing Cerezuela's
inexperience and lack of self-assertion, and asking that
the new inquisitor to be sent should be a man of
greater force. Their wishes were gratified when Antonio
Gutiérrez de Ulloa arrived, March 31, 1571. It was not
long before his arbitrary and scandalous conduct
aroused indignation, but those who dared to complain
were made to suffer. Secret information, however, was
conveyed to the Suprema and the viceroy, the Count
del Villar, was unreserved in his communications to
the king, representing that Ulloa kept spies in the
viceregal palace who carried off papers and documents,
and that he had indirectly farmed the quicksilver
mines of Guancavelica, making large sums to the detri-
ment of the royal interests. Moreover, Ulloa's promis-
cuous amours with maids and married women were
notorious; he publicly kept as a concubine Catalina
Morejón, a married woman, who used her influence to
dictate appointments and modify sentences until, after
repeated efforts, Villar succeeded in banishing her.
On one occasion a husband found him in bed with his
wife; Ulloa threatened him as inquisitor and he slunk
away; another husband was less timid, he killed the
wife and chased the adulterer through the streets. He
was in the habit of walking the streets at night dressed
as a cavalier, brawling and fighting, and on one Holy
Thursday he supped with a number of strumpets. He
and the Dominican Provincial, Fray Francisco de Val-
derrama, each had as mistress a relative of the other;
when the three years of the provincialate ended, Val-
derrama aspired to be prior of the Lima convent, but
the new Provincial, Agustín Montes, refused to appoint
him because he was a bastard, whereupon Ulloa went
to the convent, thrust a dagger to the Provincial's breast
and swore he would kill him, when Montes yielded.

He was involved in perpetual contests with the judges and royal officials, whom he treated without ceremony or justice, interfering with their functions, of which a number of cases were given which, if not exaggerated, show that the land was at the mercy of the inquisitorial officials who murdered, robbed and took women at their pleasure, and any who complained were fined or kept chained in prison.

Inquisitors of the character thus indicated, owning no superior save the distant inquisitor-general and Suprema, armed with the terrible power of excommunication which none but themselves could remove, judging all and judged by none, could not fail to be a disturbing element in the colonial administration. They were at the head of a body of officials and familiars, scattered over the land, who enjoyed exemption from all other jurisdiction, secular and ecclesiastical, and who were sure, whatever crimes they might commit, to find protection and mercy in the Tribunal. Even their servants and slaves had the benefit of this *fuero* and formed a peculiarly obnoxious class in the community. The maintenance and extension of these privileges involved the Tribunal in constant strife with the authorities, lay and spiritual, quarrels which were carried on with a violence frequently destructive to the public peace. The government officials, however high-placed, who sought to curb inquisitorial arrogance, could have slender hope of support from their royal master. There was preserved in the Madrid archives the formula of a letter addressed to viceroys, insisting on their subservience to the Inquisition. This in 1603 was duly sent to the Marquis of Monterey, viceroy of Peru. How often this was repeated it would be impossible to say, but in 1655, at least, it was sent to the Count of Alba by Philip IV, as a warning in consequence of some squabbles in which he came to be involved with the Tribunal. When the colonial Inquisitions were founded, Philip II, by a cédula of August 16, 1570, took the inquisitors and all the officials under the royal protection and decreed that anyone, no matter of what rank, who disturbed or injured them should incur the penalty of violating the safeguard, and this was repeated by Philip III in 1610.

Francisco de Toledo, the first viceroy who had to deal with the Inquisition, was a man of character who, by holding the purse-strings, managed to keep within bounds Cerezuela, who was of a yielding disposition. There was dissension, however, for which Alonso de Arceo, canon of La Plata, decried him as a heretic and a forger, whom the Tribunal dared not accuse, but when Toledo asked it to prosecute him, it evaded the request. The next viceroy, the Count del Villar, was weaker, while Ulloa, as we have seen, enforced the prerogatives of the Holy Office with a masterful hand. The quarrels which arose were long and intricate and were conducted in a way to abase thoroughly the vice-regal authority. Villar banished Catalina Morejón to put an end to the scandal of her relations with In-quisitor Ulloa; this may have been either the cause or a result of the ill-feeling between them, but motives for dissension could not be lacking when the domineer-ing spirit of the Tribunal refused obedience to all con-stituted authority, and could always frame some ex-cuse for asserting its superior jurisdiction.

It can readily be perceived how difficult was the task of the viceroys to maintain an efficient government, and to keep the peace with so independent and so unruly a factor in the land. But few of them escaped collisions. It is not surprising therefore, that, however pious were the viceroys, they were almost unanimous in deprecating the acts and the influence of the Holy Office. The Count del Villar naturally exhaled his woes in long and lugubrious epistles to the king. His successor, the Count of Cañete, as early in his term as 1589, complained bitterly of the exemptions through which all connected with the Holy Office admitted responsibility to no one. This gave rise to endless trouble, for every one who was summoned to have his accounts examined, or who refused to pay his dues to the royal treasury, procured a familiarship or some office and with it secured exemption. Even Alvaro Ruiz de Navamuel, the government secretary, had himself been made a familiar and auditor, and assumed that he was not subject to investigation. The royal officials [bureaucrats in charge of the royal treasury] were familiars —one of them at Arequipa, when called upon for his accounts, refused because he was a familiar. Government conducted after this fashion seems like *opéra bouffe*.

Even after its decadence had fairly set in, as late as 1773, the Viceroy Amat y Junient writes that the Inquisition, so necessary for the purity of the faith, would be more useful and respected if it would confine itself to its proper functions, for its cognizance of civil cases has always led to collisions with the royal courts, which are particularly prejudicial at this distance from the king and, though there have been concords and royal cédulas to prevent them, there are never lacking occasions to revive the contention to the great disquiet of the people.

The eighteenth century, in fact, presents an almost continuous series of quarrels with all the different jurisdictions, the existence of which so greatly weakened the organization of the Spanish colonial system, and these quarrels were fought out with a persistent bitterness, sometimes degenerating into violence, which taxed to the utmost the efforts of the viceroys as peacemakers.

Thus far we have considered the activity of the Tribunal in matters foreign to its purpose, which, indeed, were the most important portion of its record. As regards its proper function, that of maintaining the purity of the faith, its chief business in Peru, as in Spain, was with a class of cases which could only by forced construction be considered as heretical. Bigamists furnished a large proportion of penitents—the adventurer who left a wife in Andalusian Córdoba was apt to take a new one in Córdoba de Tucumán and chance might at any time bring detection, while, even in Peru itself, distances were so great and intercommunication so difficult, that the seeker after fortune was easily tempted in his wanderings to duplicate the sacrament of matrimony. Blasphemy was another prolific source of prosecution, for the gambling habit was universal and lost none of its provocative character in crossing the ocean. Sorcery moreover, including the innumerable superstitions for creating love or hatred, curing or causing disease, bringing fortune or averting misfortune, and foretelling the future, which were technically held to include implicit or explicit pact with the demon, brought an ample store of culprits before the Tribunal. To the mass of superstitious beliefs carried from home by the Spaniards were speedily superadded those of the native wise-women and a sprinkling taught by Guinea negro slaves. We find but few whites among these offenders, but every other caste is represented—negro, mulatto, quadroon, mestizo, and sambo and sometimes Indian, for in this crime the jurisdiction of the Inquisition over the Indians seems to have been admitted. One feature of Indian sorcery which constantly meets us is the use of the drug *peyote* which, in Mexico, was employed to produce fatidical dreams and revelations. Both of these were strictly prohibited by the respective Inquisitions.

No specific cases of witchcraft occur in the *autos da fé*, but, in 1629, a special Edict of Faith directed against the occult arts and sorcery was published, enumerating all the forbidden practices in minute detail and forming a curious body of superstitions and folklore, much more extensive than anything of the kind issued in Spain. It brought in, we are told, numerous denunciations, but the practices were ineradicable and continued to flourish until the end.

Propositions [false theological contentions], which furnished so large a portion of the work of the Spanish tribunals, afforded a much smaller percentage in Peru. This is probably attributable to lack of intellectual activity, for some of the cases tried indicate that the susceptibility of the Inquisition was as delicate as in Spain, and that there was the same readiness to denounce any careless speech or ill-sounding remark uttered in vexation or anger. Thus, in 1529, Felipe de Luján was tried because, when looking at a picture of the Last Judgement, he said it was not well painted, for Christ was not with the Apostles. Juan de Arianza had the indelible disgrace of appearing in the *auto* of February 27, 1631, because, when reading the Scriptures, he exclaimed, "Ea! there is nothing but living and dying," which sounded ill to those who heard it. A case, which came near to ending in tragedy, was that of Antonio de Campos, who, for uttering certain heretical propositions and adhering to them pertinaciously, was condemned to relaxation [commitment to the civil authorities for punishment, usually the death penalty]. Fortunately for him the expense of a public *auto* was too great to be incurred and the Suprema was consulted, in 1672. During the delay thus caused it was found that his real name was Fray Teodoro de Ribera and that his brain had been turned by a potion given him by a woman. This afforded a solution and he was handed over as insane to this provincial.

One of the most frequent offenses, not strictly heretical, with which the Inquisition had to deal, was that of so-called solicitation—the seduction of women by priests in the confessional, but as these offenders never appear in the relations of the *autos*, they are only to be gathered from more or less imperfect records. Prior to 1578 there had been various cases, about one of which, that of Antonio Hernández de Villaroel, the Tribunal reported that it could not diminish the penalty of perpetual deprivation of confessing women, because this had been ordered by the Suprema in the case of Rodrigo de Arcos, and this was construed as a general law. If so, it was not long in force for, about 1580, we find Juan de Alarcón deprived for only three years. In a collection of cases between 1578 and 1581 there are seven of solicitation and between 1581 and 1585 there are eight. Thus they are constantly appearing and, in 1595, we are told that there were twenty-four priests in prison awaiting sentence, one of whom, Juan de Figueroa, was testified against by forty-three women. In 1597 seven priests were prosecuted from the province of Tucumán alone, where, among the Indian converts, few confessors seem to have had scruples.

In view of the heinousness of the offence the treatment of culprits in Spain was remarkably lenient, but this was surpassed by the tenderness shown to them in Peru. Another fraile from Tucumán, the Dominican Francisco Vázquez, was sentenced in 1599 for this and for twenty-four scandalous propositions, but for this cumulation of offences he escaped with deprivation of confessing women and reclusion for a year in a convent. At the same time the Franciscan Bartolomé de la Cruz, guardian of the convent at Santiago de Estero, against whom fifteen women testified, was deprived of confessing and had some spiritual penances. Fray Andrés Corral, guardian of the convent of Las Juntas, testified against by twenty-eight women, had aggravated the offense by committing rape in the church and for this he was banished from Tucumán and subjected to discipline. On the other hand Rodrigo Ortiz Melgarejo, the only priest in Asunción, denounced himself to the commissioner in 1594, to the delegate in Asunción and to the Tribunal in 1596, for guilt with seven women. He was obliged to go to Lima, where he presented himself in 1600. He was regarded as excessively scrupulous, he had performed a journey of over a thousand miles and this seems to have been thought an ample punishment.

In some of these cases the customary reading of the sentences before colleagues of the culprits was omitted because, as the Tribunal explained, there were so many of them of various orders that the omission seemed best to spare the honor of the religious bodies; the character of the Indian female witnesses was doubtful, but experience showed they spoke the truth, for most of the accused confessed and this was confirmed by the evil lives and example of all the frailes summoned from Tucumán. This had led the Tribunal to deprive them perpetually of confessing women, even when the witnesses were Indians and few in number, especially as all those priests and frailes were very ignorant and profligate.

The most serious business of the Tribunal, in the line of its proper functions, was with the apostasy of the Jewish New Christians. From the very foundation of the colonies, restrictions were laid on the emigration of *conversos* [Jews recently converted to Christianity] and a law of 1543, preserved in the *Recopilación*, orders that search be made for all descendants of Jews who were to be rigorously expelled. In spite, however, of the jealous care observed to preserve the colonies from all danger of Jewish infection, the commercial attractions were so powerful that the New Christians eluded all precautions.

With regard to the general character of the punishments inflicted it may be remarked that they vary capriciously, in accordance doubtless with the temper of the inquisitors, whose discretion had few limits. In the earlier days there would seem to be a tendency to greater rigor than that customary in Spain. In the *auto* of 1578 the sentences, as a rule, are exceedingly severe. When Judaism came to be conspicuous, the penalties which we have seen inflicted were very similar to those imposed for the same offense by the home Tribunals. As the galleys went out of fashion and were replaced by forced labor in the *presidios*, the principal destination to which culprits were sent was Valdivia, though occasionally they were assigned to Callao, Chagre, or other ports where fortifications were under construction. Scourging, as in Spain, was a favorite resort, without distinction of sex. In the *auto* of 1736 there were sixteen sentences of two hundred lashes, half of them on women, for bigamy, sorcery and other similar offenses. In addition to the suffering, there was the severest of humiliations for those sensitive to shame. The so-called penitents were marched in procession through the streets, naked from the waist up, with insignia or inscriptions denoting their offenses, while the executioner plied the lash. The assembled mob was in the habit of manifesting its piety by stoning the poor wretches, to repress which the Tribunal occasionally issued a proclamation. Before the *auto* of October 19, 1749, it forbade the throwing of stones, apples, oranges or other missiles at the penitents, under pain of a hundred pesos for Spaniards and ten pesos with four days of prison for others. Exile was a frequent penalty, sometimes to a designated place, but more frequently from certain cities or districts, where the culprit had committed offenses; when this happened to be his native home, where his trade or profession was established, it might be a most severe infliction, depriving him of his means of livelihood; when the culprit was a vagrant or an old sorceress it mattered little.

Not the least important function of the Inquisition was the censorship of the press. Although in Spain this was reserved to the Suprema, and the tribunals could only refer to it books which they regarded as suspect, distance rendered independent action necessary in the colonies. From an early period the Lima tribunal examined books and prohibited such as it saw fit. The importation of printed matter was also, as in Spain, subject to its supervision. The original instructions, borne by Cerezuela, enjoined special watchfulness by the commissioners at the seaports, to prevent the introduction of all works that were on the *Index*. To insure this, at first no books were admitted except through Callao, and the commissioner at Panama was required to keep a close watch on everything destined for that point. Nothing could be shipped from there without his license, nor could any package be opened except in his presence. The same vigilance was exercised at Callao, and all books were sent to Fray Juan de Almaraz, prior of San Agustín, for examination. As the settlement and commerce of Buenos Aires developed, similar precautions were observed there. There was always a haunting dread of the efforts attributed to the Protestants to smuggle books into the land. In 1605 there was a scare of this kind, based on rumors that ships from Lisbon manned by Flemings were bringing such works in casks purporting to contain wine or salt, and special orders were issued to the commissioner to be doubly watchful. As in Spain, this system was a serious impediment to trade, and led not infrequently to collisions with the secular authorities. It required that all ships on arrival should be visited by the commissioner before any passenger or merchandise was landed, and that the latter, when brought on shore, should be opened in his presence and minutely inspected.

Even so high an ecclesiastical dignitary as the Archbishop of Lima was not exempt from the censorship of the Tribunal. Juan de Almoguera, who was archbishop from 1674 to 1676, while yet bishop of Arequipa, had been strongly impressed with the dissolute lives of the priests among the Indians and, in 1671, he published in Madrid a series of Instructions, which the inquisitors held to be not only defamatory to the priests, but to contain propositions adverse to the Holy See. The archbishop defended himself by asserting that his doctrines were approved by the more learned men of Peru, and that the facts which he cited were perfectly true, for which he appealed to the testimony of the inquisitors themselves. They admitted this, but nevertheless they caused the edict of prohibition to be published everywhere.

The reformatory legislation of Carlos III, from 1762 to 1768, limiting the unrestricted control of the Inquisition over the prohibition of books, was long in reaching Peru. In 1773 Viceroy Amat y Junient says that although he had not yet received the cédula of 1768 officially through the Council of the Indies, yet he defines its provisions as a guide. It put in force the Constitution *Sollicita ac provida* of Benedict XIV, entitling authors to be heard in defense of their books; it prevented the prohibition of books *ad interim* until a final decision was reached; where expurgations were ordered they were to be made known so that owners could delete the objectionable passages, and all edicts were to be submitted to the viceroy before publication.

The demand for literature must have been greater than would have been anticipated, for, in 1772, there was a discussion between the viceroy and the Tribunal over the proceedings in opening and examining 165 cases of books.

At this period, the censorship was exercised largely through the civil authorities. February 28, 1787, the Viceroy Count de Croix reported to the king the execution of his orders of 1785 in the suppression and burning of certain books, the seizure of all copies that could be traced to the possession of booksellers or of individuals, and the issue of an edict prohibiting the printing of anything without a license, even the University not being permitted to publish the eulogies and addresses customary on the arrival of a viceroy, or the Latin orations with which the studies were annually opened. The Inquisition is only alluded to in connection with the examination of importations, none being delivered from the custom-house without preliminary inspection by the commissioner of the Tribunal, in connection with an appointee of the government. As in Spain, this censorship extended over morals as well as over religion and politics. In 1796, Antonio Ortiz, the commissioner of Buenos Aires, was much exercised over certain wall-papers received from Barcelona. Some of them had mythological figures, such as Hercules, Venus and the like, which he considered intolerable. There was another one representing the globe adorned with flowers and presided over by Cupid with a lighted torch, as though to burn it with his impure fires, all of which he was compelled to cut up into small pieces.

In the turbulent atmosphere of the early nineteenth century, the authority of the Inquisition naturally declined, especially as the character of the inquisitors was so unfitted to inspire respect. Its suppression by the decree of the Cortes of Cádiz, February 22, 1813, was evidently seen in advance to be inevitable and was fatal to its influence.

The total amount of work accomplished is estimated by José Toribio Medina as three thousand cases tried, but this is probably too liberal an allowance. His exhaustive researches have resulted only in an enumeration of 1474 cases.

For the 250 years of existence, the estimate of a total of 3000 cases would make 12 per annum, or 1 per month, but in the first 20 years of the tribunal the cases amounted to 1265, which would reduce the average of the other 230 years to about 7½, and it would be safe to assume for the last century an average of not more than 3 or 4 a year.

For this slender result, to say nothing of the large expenditure, the colony was kept in a constant state of disquiet, the orderly course of government was well-nigh impossible, intellectual, commercial and industrial development were impeded, universal distrust of one's neighbor was commanded by ordinary prudence, and the population lived with the sense of evil ever impending over the head of every one. That there was any real danger to the faith in Peru is absurd. Possibly the Tribunal may have been of some service in repressing the prevalence of bigamy among laymen and of solicitation among the clergy, but the fact that these two offenses remained to the last so prominent in its calendar would show that it accomplished little. In the repression of the practices which were regarded as implying pact with the demon, the Inquisition may be said to have virtually accomplished nothing. It would be difficult to find, in the annals of human misgovernment, a parallel case in which so little was accomplished at so great a cost as by the Inquisition under Spanish institutions.

SALVADOR DE MADARIAGA

The Church and the Inquisition in the Spanish American Colonies

Since the early years of the twentieth century, an important revision in the interpretation of colonial Ibero-American history has been underway in the United States and England. A fundamental aspect of this revisionist movement has been the recognition of the many laudable achievements of Spain and Portugal in America. Salvador de Madariaga has made a significant contribution toward instructing the English-speaking world about the brighter aspects of Iberian colonial activities in the New World. Although born in Spain in 1886, Madariaga has probably exercised his greatest influence in England. As early as 1928 the eminent diplomat-author served as professor of Spanish Studies at Oxford University. With some interruptions, he has continued his teaching and research career in England. Many of his more than twenty books were written in that country and originally published there or in the United States.

HOW about the things of the mind? It goes without saying that they flourished within the bosom of the Church and in the light of the faith. It is difficult for persons born and bred in an era of free enquiry to imagine what life can have been in an era of orthodoxy; most difficult of all, to realize how free the mind felt

Reprinted with permission of the Macmillan Company and A. P. Watt and Son from *The Rise of the Spanish American Empire*, by Salvador de Madariaga. Copyright 1947 by Salvador de Madariaga. Excerpts from pp. 142-168.

within an orthodoxy so consubstantial with it as to become part of its life. This and only this can explain why the Crown of Spain in the heyday of the Inquisition upheld . . . freedom of conscience. "Amongst other things,"—writes Philip II to his Ambassador at the Court of Elizabeth—"you may say that they cannot fairly refuse the request about the Churches [asking that churches be maintained for English Catholics] as even the Turk allows the Christians who live in his country to worship God in their own way." This from the Philip who, in the same letter, instructs his Ambassador to watch all Spanish heretics in England and Flanders, and to report their doings to the Holy Office. Similarly, during the protracted negotiations towards the marriage of Charles I, when Prince of Wales, to a Spanish Infanta, Gondomar repeatedly stated in London that the consent of Philip III would never be given unless James I granted "freedom of conscience" in his kingdom to all his subjects. "I have read many times Y. M.'s instructions on this subject"—writes Gondomar to Philip III—"and find that without liberty of conscience the marriage cannot be agreed to." No insincerity should be read into this attitude, due merely to the fact that the faith (i.e., their faith) was for these men a matter of substance, not of opinion, and that, therefore, they were unaware of the absurd contradiction which their stand implied. Paradoxical as this may sound to us liberty of thought for the Spaniards of the sixteenth and seventeenth centuries was perfectly compatible with orthodoxy. The heretic? Why, he was so obviously in error, that no one could call "that" thought. The trouble was not the heretic, but the bordercase. And it did not come from the principle of the Holy Office, but from its corruption at the hands of self-seeking, passionate, narrow-minded or petty churchmen.

The Spanish Church in the sixteenth century was a great, noble and creative institution. Yet in the course of time it deteriorated in the fatherland, and as economic (as well as spiritual) success accrued to the

Church in the Indies, it fell from its original evangelical zeal and purity. The records of the Inquisition of Lima show how rapidly the Church fell down the slippery path of wealth and lust. The number of priests and monks who have to answer for the gravest sins against chastity is appalling. To judge by some of the cases, the ecclesiastical authorities were lenient towards the evil; the Inquisition less so, though by no means as rigid as in matters of dogma; and again, it was the Crown which took the sternest attitude.

This evolution of the Spanish Church from evangelical purity to corrupt refinement must be borne in mind if the much discussed Inquisition is to be appraised in its true historical perspective. It is here, perhaps, that the fog of prejudice which darkens and deforms the plainest facts of Spanish history is thickest.

There was a procession of sixteen victims with ropes around their necks, including six priests, a lawyer, and a merchant, the sentences being two hundred lashes on some, burning on others, confiscation on all. The next *auto da fé* was in 1581, when there were twenty victims, and so the ghastly work continued during the centuries of Spanish domination, creating a sensation of terror through the land, spreading misery and sorrow broadcast, benumbing thought, and gradually, but very surely, exciting hatred and repulsion.*

This is the kind of solemn nonsense which still passes for History. That word "victims"; that terror spread, that thought benumbed, that hatred and repulsion—and that oblivion of conditions elsewhere—all contribute to create an impression of reality which bears no relation whatsover to reality itself. First as to victims. "The next *auto da fé*"—we are told—"was in 1581, when there were twenty victims, and so the ghastly work continued. . . ." What happened in 1581? One man, Juan Bernal, who would not adjure Lutheranism, was burnt alive. The other nineteen "vic-

* Clements Markham, *History of Peru*, p. 171, quoted by Bernard Moses, *South America on the Eve of the Emancipation* (New York, 1908), p. 15.

tims," guilty of either unorthodox opinions, or bigamy, or sexual offenses (when priests) were sentenced to the galleys, to prison for life or for a number of years, to exile, to one hundred lashes and so forth. Such are the facts. In the whole of the Indies, for the whole three centuries of Spanish rule, the number of fatal victims of the Inquisition, including those who committed suicide or went mad under the physical or moral torture which an antiquated and benighted system entailed, stands nearer to sixty than to one hundred. Let us put it at thirty a century on an average. Thirty victims a century for a whole continent and for a population as large as that of England and Spain put together; when in England alone, and only under the Tudors, the victims of religious persecution on both sides exceed five hundred. From our modern point of view the Inquisition cannot be defended in itself. But to single it out from the practices and ideas of the day as "the" institution of persecution and cruelty is unhistorical.*

Witch-hunting became almost a sport in Germany. In Trier, during the second half of the sixteenth century,

. . . inasmuch as it was popularly believed that the continued sterility of many years was caused by witches through the malice of the Devil, the whole country rose to exterminate the witches. This movement was promoted by many in office who hoped for wealth from the persecution. And so, from Court to Court throughout the towns and villages of all the Diocese, scurried special accusers, inquisitors, notaries, jurors, judges, constables, dragging to trial and torture human beings of both sexes and burning them in great numbers [. . .] So far, at length, did the madness of the furious populace and of the Courts go in this thirst for blood and booty that there was scarcely anybody who was not smirched by some suspicion

---

* On the Inquisition [says Madariaga at this point], rather than Lea, who is hopelessly biased, one must trust José Torbio Medina,—who, although not very intelligent, is most conscientious. [The editor suggests that the reader consult for a more laudatory appraisal of Medina's level of competence on Inquisition research Maury A. Bromsen, editor, *José Toribio Medina, Humanist of the Americas* (Washington, D.C., 1960)].

of this crime. Meanwhile, notaries, copyists and innkeepers grew rich. The executioner rode a blooded horse, like a noble of the Court. [. . .] The children of the convicted and punished were sent into exile; their goods confiscated; plowman and vintner failed. . . .

The number of victims in Germany must have risen to tens of thousands. In England the figure has been put as high as 70,000 for those executed under the Act of James I—a figure probably in excess by nine-tenths. The more moderate and, it seems, competent estimate, puts the number of executions for witchcraft in England between 1543 and 1736 at just short of one thousand. England had then a population rather less than one-third of that of the Indies. Therefore England hanged proportionately thirty to fifty times more persons for witchcraft than the Spanish Inquisition in the Indies burned for heresy.

In 1692 nineteen witches were hanged at Salem in New England. One was pressed to death. Eight more condemned. Fifty confessed themselves witches and were pardoned. One hundred and fifty were imprisoned, above two hundred accused, and many fled the country to save their lives. No wonder that

these good people in New England have had perhaps as large Experience of these Matters as any; and in the midst of their Confusions, their Clergy had a Meeting at the Desire of their Magistrates, to give their Opinion in several cases proposed to them: and the Question was, *Whether Satan may not appear in the Shape of an innocent and pious, as well as of an innocent and wicked Person, to afflict such as suffer by Diabolical Molestation?* And they returned it as their Opinion, *That he might*; and confirmed it not only by Examples of other Times and Places, but by what they had seen amongst themselves.

Not till these facts are borne in mind and a general picture of the period emerges in all its grim features, is it possible to realize that, while cruel, superstitious and benighted, as all its epoch was, the Inquisition was on the whole less cruel, less superstitious and less benighted than the average practice of the age elsewhere;

and that it concentrated on dogma and behaviour rather than on the grossly superstitious persecutions of poor wretches accused of witchcraft.

The Spanish Inquisition did not usually punish witch-craft with death. Indeed, it seems to have looked upon it as a crime to be branded more with ridicule. In the *auto da fé* held in Mexico on December 8th, 1598, there were seven persons convicted of witchcraft—all women. They were all sentenced to "*auto*, candle and cone hood, abjuration *de levi* and exiled from Mexico," and all but one to sums varying between 100 and 400 pesos. Only one was sentenced to flogging—two hundred lashes. None to either prison or death.

The uselessness, the trouble, the worry, the waste of life and money, the agony caused in the families of the prosecuted, the economic and social chaos caused by confiscations and the cruelty of the methods applied to extort confessions are matters of common knowl-edge. Yet, strange as it may sound, the emotions raised by the facts and the wholesale historical distortion of four centuries of biased History have concentrated on the cruelty of the Inquisition which, given the age, was no special feature at all, to the neglect of its true vice—corruption. This double error comes from the fact that the Holy Office in the Indies (as in Spain) has been generally considered out of its true, biological context.

To begin with, though it was unspeakably cruel and stupid, it was on the whole mild and progressive in rela-tion to the standards of the period. Its tortures were appalling but they were what it found in use and it did not innovate. Nothing, for instance, to compare with the *bootkins* used in Scotland, nor with the abominable way in which the "water-cure" was used in our own lifetime under American authorities; while its standards of prison life were far in advance over anything known anywhere at the time. The proportion of death sen-tences to prosecutions was about one in a hundred. Witchcraft prosecutions in England (where the Courts were far less strict than in Scotland) led to the gal-lows in 19 cases out of 100; and in 41 per cent of the cases during the first four years of James I's reign. During the summer of 1645, the campaign launched by the famous "witchfinder," Hopkins, cost the life of 19 out of 29 women prosecuted. Even if, to the cases of death by execution for which the Inquisition was responsible in the Indies, we add those of physical suffering which sometimes entailed death, it is plain that the Holy Office in the Indies, though responsible for much suffering, cannot be said to count as one of the chief agencies of torment in History, particularly if it is borne in mind that life in those three centuries was cheap and cruelty rampant everywhere. The Inquisition cost less lives to the whole of the Indies in three centuries than were lost in one week in Carnival brawls among the rich and rowdy inhabitants of Potosí.

The Holy Office was bad enough, in a way, though not in that in which it is usual to present "the Inquisition." But the picture of "terror, misery, sorrow, hatred and repulsion," painted by Markham, Lea and others is a pure illusion. The Inquisition, despite the terrible sufferings of those who did suffer at its hands, did no more to spread gloom and sorrow in the Indies than religious persecution or witch-hunting in merrie England, where the flowing of blood by no means interfered with, rather did it stimulate, the flowing of beer. The Inquisition was both human and inhuman—like the whole world of its day . . . and of ours. Moreover, it was popular, all too popular. There was in it more social gossip, more envy, more of the many small spices of the stew of life than the deep sounding gloom of tragedy often associated with its name.

"Juan de la Parra, born in this capital," wrote the Inquisition of Lima to the Supreme Council in Madrid,

was arrested and given a sentence in this Holy Office as an observer of the law of Moses and took part in an *auto* in 1661. In later days he made a fortune, married and he has many children, and gradually took to ostentatious ways for himself and his family, with a carriage, hangings in his house, always riding about, though on a mule, which is here the habit, dressed in silk, he, his wife and all his children, with the usual ornaments of pearls and diamonds which one generally sees on persons of the first quality. With these demonstrations and others, and some vanity, he gave occasion for the Holy Office to take note of everything, and as it was proved that he had not obtained a licence to do any of the things which had been forbidden him in his sentence, he was summoned and the sentence was notified to him afresh, ordering him to keep to it, with a number of warnings; he was fined two thousand pesos. He obeyed forthwith without objection.

The jealousy of the neighbors richer in orthodoxy and poorer in silk and pearls can be seen here at play in the corridors of the Holy Office. This small change of daily events kept the popularity of the Inquisition ever alive; and when it organized its *autos* the pageant was always carefully regulated, and everyone in the city was eager to take part in it.

At the appointed hour many honourable citizens congregated in the hope that each would be entrusted with a penitent whom he would accompany in the *auto*, thus showing in every way they could the affection with which they desired to serve the Holy Office. But [. . .] it so happened that Don Salvador Velázquez, a noble Indian, Chief Sergeant of the Militia of Natives, arrived at the Holy Office at the same time as the other [Spanish] citizens, in his best uniform, with a sword and a silver dagger, and he asked to be honoured with the duty of conveying one of the effigies which were to go in the *auto*, for that was his purpose; and in view of his eagerness, it was granted to him and also to one of his companions.

Where is the terror and the gloom? What in actual fact was the chief crime of the Inquisition was that it failed to maintain the standards which it professed to serve: the purity of the faith and the decency of behaviour. Many of its officials, high and low, became corrupt (here again, it would seem, more so in Peru than in New Spain). The records are full of the undignified squabbles between the various officials of the actual tribunal and of its bureaucracy, due mostly to the lowest motives of self interest, at times to rivalry about women, despite their ecclesiastical profession, and often to puerile incidents over precedence in which the ministers of the Holy Office were constantly disputing first rank to the *oidores* of the *audiencia*. Inquisitors speculated with the money of the Holy Office and waxed rich thereon, took mistresses and dressed like young bloods in silk and lace. Poison and arson were at times resorted to in order to get rid of rivals or documents.

What was at fault was not the doctrine, which, within the limitations of the period was not too unreasonable. In judging the Inquisition of those days, we have no right to expect modern standards of scientific knowledge. Even so, in what concerns, for instance, prediction of events and the relations between astrology and astronomy, the Inquisition was singularly wise and in advance of its time. Eminent European astronomers, whose names shine in the annals of science, believed in astrology. Tycho Brahe, for one. The Inquisition did not, and when Lima went through an epidemic of illuminations, visions and revelations, the Holy Office of Peru nailed to church doors a remarkable document in which the orthodox view against judiciary astrology is defined as follows: "There is no human art or science capable of manifesting the things which are to come, when they are dependent on the will of man, for this has been reserved by God our Lord to Himself, with His eternal wisdom." Note how the field of scientific previsibility is respected by the Holy Office.

The case of Sarmiento de Gamboa is typical in this respect. He was a Spaniard of Gallegan and Basque blood, "well versed in astronomy." But there is no doubt that he dabbled in magic. It was noticed that he wore specially engraved rings to which he attributed magic powers. He had given one of these rings to the Don-Juanesque Count of Nieva, the viceroy, for he attributed to it the power of winning women's graces. The Inquisition took a hand in the matter, and the viceroy rescued the magician by sending him "to discover" in the South Seas. He discovered the Solomon

Islands (1567). When he returned to Lima, Don Francisco de Toledo was already in office. The new viceroy undertook a personal survey of Peru, and chose Sarmiento de Gamboa as his assistant, to set down "the descriptions and book of tables of the things of the Indies" and he later wrote to the king that he had "finished to wander about this land with the ablest man in these matters whom I have found in it." But the incorrigible Sarmiento took then to chiromancy and was again in difficulties with the Inquisition. Again he was rescued by the viceroy on the ground that he was needed to chart the Magellan Straits (1579), just rediscovered by Drake. This fact, the sending of Sarmiento, was sung in verse in the next century:

> *He sailed to cross the fiery plans of Drake.*

The author of the poem, Peralta Barnuevo, was a kind of Peruvian Sarmiento. Born in Lima (1663) he was a doctor of medicine, an astronomer, a military engineer, a musician, and a poet, though bad. He wrote *Lima Inexpugnable*, tried to make it so, translated Corneille, printed astronomical tables, wrote for the theater and published books in Greek, Latin, Italian, French, Portuguese and Castilian, all of which languages he is said to have mastered. But when very old he bethought himself to write a treatise on *Pasión y Triunfo de Cristo*, and, of course, got into trouble with the Inquisition. Yet again in this case, the Viceroy, Marqués de Castellfuerte, intervened and he died in peace in 1743.

The viceroys are therefore often if not constantly seen on the side of tolerance, and protecting men of mental value against the Holy Office. But on the other hand, it does not appear that the Holy Office persecuted men who kept to their scientific path and did not stray into either magic or theology. The most remarkable case of all is perhaps that of Nicholas Legras or Bandier, who was sentenced to abjuration and exile; a picturesque figure, a kind of Rabelais, priest and doctor, whose views were those of a modern freethinker and agnostic. Now this man had come to Peru in the household of the Viceroy, Count of Santisteban (1661) as his doctor and tutor of his son; and he did not get into trouble with the Inquisition till after the Viceroy's death in 1666. The witnesses for the prosecution were an Englishman and three Frenchmen. "The republic and people of Lima"—one reads in the proceedings— "were very uneasy against this man, so that even persons of virtue and capacity were getting ready to kill him if he came out into the street." Here again is the theme of the popularity of the Holy Office in the Indies. The Peruvian Peralta Barnuevo sang its praises in prose, and the Chilean Pedro de Oña in verse.

Oh pure, sublime, straightforward Holy Office!

The tone was, up to a point, that of official laudation. The unseemly life of many an Inquisitor was bound to detract from the dignity and respect due to the Tribunal. Nevertheless, the Holy Office kept its prestige intact with many of the learned, and its popularity alive with the masses, particularly in the capitals such as Lima and Mexico, where its processions and *autos da fé* were eagerly awaited festivals. The historical superstitions which still prevail over those *autos da fé* stand in the way of an adequate understanding of what they really meant for the people. The fiery stake was not always set alight, and when it was, only for one or two victims and not in the town, nor by the Holy Office, nor as a part of the *auto da fé*. For an *auto da fé*, as its name implies, was an act of faith. And those who made an act of faith, unless they were relapses, i.e., men who had already been given a chance, were not sentenced to death. Executions of relapses which were always handed over to the civic authority, were relished by the populace, just as executions have ever been at all times and in all places. The run today in London, Paris or New York to witness an execution if the authorities allowed it would be terrific. Blood and scaffold fiends were not less keen in every other crowd than in Spanish or Spanish Indian crowds, and the sight was,

if possible, less ghastly in the case of executions decreed
by the Inquisition than in the usual forms of death
under European or English criminal law.

The *auto da fé* was above all a pageant of human
drama and of colour—human drama because rich and
poor alike, when guilty, could be seen under the eyes
of poor and rich pass in the procession humbled and
crushed under the weight of error and sin; colour, because the ceremonies—processions and sittings—were
carefully staged sights, with the purple silk of the
bishops, the black, white, brown and blue gowns of the
monks, the scarlet velvets and blue damasks of viceroys
and high officials, the red sashes garnished with silver
of the military, the noble curves of the richly capari-
soned horses, the shrill note of the silver clarions, and
the solemn green cross of the Inquisition rising above
the rows of candles which shone like feeble stars trembling in the sun. The Inquisition was a part of that
strange and wonderful life of the Indies, one of the rare
periods of History which have succeeded in creating
that elusive virtue—a style.

IRVING A. LEONARD

Visitas and Books

Irving A. Leonard, Domingo Faustino Sarmiento University Professor of Spanish American History and Literature at the University of Michigan, has engaged in extensive research on the reading preferences and habits of the Spanish colonists. He has also studied closely the intellectual milieu in general. In the several books which he has written, he shows that in spite of restrictive laws, the actual intellectual environment was characterized by extensive freedom. The following selection stresses the ineffectiveness of the Inquisition and suggests that its officials exercised considerably less than absolute control over the intellectual pursuits of the colonists.

THE profound conviction of both the Crown and the Church that the propagation of the Catholic faith in the newly acquired realms must be safeguarded at all costs from the schismatic dissensions of contemporary Europe stimulated their unremitting, if somewhat unsuccessful, efforts to prevent the circulation of heretical books in the Indies. These rulers made earnest attempts not only to choke off the exportation of such literature from Spain itself but also to exclude from entrance to the ports of debarkation any works of subversive character which might evade the vigilance of the officials in the homeland. The preventive measure

Reprinted by permission of the publishers and the author, from Irving A. Leonard, *Books of the Brave: Being an Account of Books and Men in the Spanish Conquest and Settlement of the Sixteenth-Century New World,* Cambridge, Mass.: Harvard University Press, copyright 1949, by the President and Fellows of Harvard College. (Excerpts from p. 166-182.)

adopted for the American side of the Atlantic service was a *visita*, or customs inspection, of all incoming ships. A decree of 1556 required the treasury officers at these terminal points to exercise extreme care in checking the cargoes of arriving vessels with the sealed registers they brought in order to note the possible inclusion of books on the Inquisition *Index*; any listed works discovered must be turned over promptly to the archbishops or their duly appointed representatives. The lax enforcement of this command—the fate of so many in the sixteenth century and later—soon obliged the authorities to consider the establishment of a special agency to perform this and other functions, since the menace of heresy was growing alarmingly. Thus it was decided to install in the New World itself branches of the secular arm of the Church, known as the Holy Office of the Inquisition, to supervise and coordinate all activities designed to protect the purity and integrity of the one True Faith.

Until 1570 the inquisitorial powers in the colonies rested mainly in the hands of the archbishops or their appointed subordinates. Prior to this date there was some censorial activity but it was, on the whole, sporadic and unsystematic. The Lutheran revolt in Europe was spreading even as the *conquistadores* were overrunning the New World and as the pioneer missionaries were attempting the spiritual conquest of its aboriginal inhabitants. The long-drawn-out sessions of the historic Council of Trent, which met intermittently from 1545 to 1563, were dominated by the ultra-conservative elements of the Church, and hence they failed to arrive at any formulae of reconciliation with the dissident Protestants. The great schism widened as official Spanish Catholicism clung fanatically to a rigid orthodoxy which inevitably placed it on the defensive. In an effort to purify itself within its doctrinal frame and to exclude what were regarded as pernicious influences, it resorted to practices of censorship which, on the whole, proved more potent for evil than for good. In the last of its long sessions the Council of

Trent drew up a series of ten rules "as a guide and instruction for all ecclesiastics or other authorities who might thereafter be charged with the duty of literary censorship." These laws applied to theological and religious works almost exclusively, though the seventh commandment dealing with "books professedly treating of lascivious or obscene subjects, or narrating, or teaching these" clearly opened the door to banning secular literature of a lighter character.

The increasing dread of Protestantism and the fear of heretical books steadily invading the overseas dominions of Spain spurred a prompt compliance with the directives of both secular and ecclesiastical councils, but the machinery of enforcement was invariably defective. To remedy the situation inquisitional tribunals similar to those existing in Spain were authorized for the colonies, and they began to operate in Lima and Mexico City on January 29, 1570, and on November 4, 1571, respectively. It was anticipated that these local branches would be more efficient in hunting down and eradicating growing evils. Books immediately claimed the special attention of the transplanted Inquisition, but only those works, it should be emphasized, which were regarded as so inimical to the faith or to good morals that they gained a place on the official *Index*. The bishops in the viceroyalties had had some discretion in discharging their duties of this sort and they were occasionally arbitrary, but their interference with the circulation of books other than those officially proscribed by the home office of the Inquisition in Spain was infrequent. Indeed, these high dignitaries showed a surprising indifference to the literature of recreation, considering the tirades directed against it during the sixteenth century from their own pulpits and the fact that these *"libros profanos"* were specifically and repeatedly prohibited in the Spanish Indies by secular decrees of the Crown.

On January 3, 1570, Dr. Pedro Moya de Contreras, then serving as Inquisitor of Murcia in the Peninsula, was notified of his designation as presiding executive of

the projected Tribunal at Mexico City. Though he
started for the New World late that year, delays of one
sort or another, including shipwreck off the coast of
Cuba, prevented him from setting up this new branch
of the Holy Office until near the end of 1571. One of
his first official acts was to publish a long edict which
stipulated, among other matters, that booksellers and
private persons receiving shipments of printed material
from Spain must present invoices or lists for the scrutiny of the Inquisition before claiming delivery. After
this checking the owners would receive instructions on
the disposition they could make of their books.

The bureaucratic meddling with individual enterprise, theretofore relatively unrestricted, promptly drew
the fire of a small group of bookdealers of Mexico
City. The commissioner of the Inquisition had stopped
delivery of a shipment of breviaries and missals, and the
aggrieved merchants protested that this act was an
obvious injustice and amounted to a virtual confiscation of their property. This incident was symptomatic
of the conflicts and disagreements which disturbed
the relations of the representatives of the State, the
Holy Office, and the commercial elements throughout
the colonial period, and these irritations largely nullified the carefully devised efforts of authorities, ecclesiastical and secular alike, to control contraband and
the black-market operations of the period. The first
point of contact where friction developed was at the
port of entry on the occasion of the customs inspection,
which was aggravated by the separate inquisitorial
visita.

Earlier royal decrees had required specially appointed treasury officials to inspect for the Crown all
incoming ships, whether single or in fleets, at the terminal ports of the Indies. No goods or persons could go
ashore until this indispensable formality was completed.
The inspectors must uncover by careful search any
unregistered goods and detect any unlicensed persons
seeking entry into the colonies. Carelessness, indifference and, probably as often, flagrant corruption charac-

terized the execution of these commands. The task of
opening all the containers in the cargoes, checking
their contents, and closing them again was too labo-
rious and time-consuming, and it delayed far too long
the disembarkation of sea-weary travelers. The crews
and officers naturally resented such excessive exertions
at the end of a tiring voyage, and the merchants were
disgruntled by the resulting disarrangement of their
wares. And, in the end, all this bother did not stop
petty thieving, fraud, or contraband. Soon the more
convenient method was instituted of summoning sailors, officers, and passengers on deck and demanding
from them an oral statement under oath. This procedure saved a vast amount of trouble, but lent itself
even more effectively to evasion and deceit; swearing
to the truth of an allegation quickly became mechanical
and in no way prevented private deals by faithless officials with merchants and peddlers on the incoming
vessels. With such malpractices general, contraband
trade flourished even before the Conquistador had
finished his work in the New World, and these abuses
largely nullified the carefully contrived regulations governing commerce and navigation between Spain and
its colonies.

Considering the opportunities for private gain enjoyed by the Crown inspectors and the merchants alike,
the evident resentment and hostility of both to the
added inquisitorial *visita* are understandable. A parallel
inspection for ecclesiastical purposes had various disad-
vantages. In the first place, it amounted to a division of
authority, and the treasury officials were always jealous
of their prerogatives, but more important still, it
meant a menace to or, at least, a sharing of the illicit
traffic they found so remunerative. Consequently, the
second and concurrent *visita* intended to ferret out
prohibited books and images thus instituted by the
newly appointed Inquisitor created a new source of
conflict, wrangling, and confusion in the disorder associated with the arrival of the fleet and the period during
which the ships remained in port. The effect of this

situation is reflected in the frequency with which the Holy Office urged its representatives at Vera Cruz to exercise the utmost tact in their dealings with their fellow inspectors, the treasury officials of the Crown, and to take extreme care in restoring books and other objects examined to the original cases and in such good condition that their owners should have no legitimate cause for complaint. The fear of vexing merchants, clearly evident in these written orders of the Inquisition, indicates that this dread institution did not enjoy the oppressive sway over all elements of colonial society traditionally ascribed to it.

When the General of a fleet put into port his first duty was to notify the customs officers of the Crown stationed there and then stand by until their work was done. Both the secular and the inquisitorial inspectors were cautioned by their respective superiors to be punctual in meeting the fleets and individual vessels so that the debarkation of passengers and freight should be delayed as little as possible—another indication of the healthy respect that the allegedly tyrannical Crown and Church had for the business elements of the colonial society over which these authorities are presumed to have exercised despotic sway. Both of the delegations put out from the shore in small boats provided by the government and soon they clambered up the sides of the anchored ships. Since the books of the Conquistador and his descendants are of primary interest here, only the routine of the inquisitorial *visita* will be described.

Accompanying the deputy of the Holy Office were a notary and an *alguacil*, or constable, or occasionally a fellow official of the Inquisition who bore its emblem of authority. Into the stern cabin or some other these inspectors summoned the shipmaster, the pilot, and one or two passengers, who represented all the rest. In the absence of the latter, since some of the ships conveyed merely freight or slaves, a pair of the more intelligent members of the crew were brought together and each one of this group was constrained to answer eight

questions and to swear to speak the truth, under penalty
of the severest anathema of the Church.

If nothing worthy of note developed out of this
cross-examination, the deputy with his assistant and
the notary were to search the stern cabin and others he
thought necessary; he should have a few boxes, chests,
or bales opened that might possibly conceal banned
books or other prohibited articles since it was the
"ordinary fashion of heretics" to smuggle printed volumes among legitimate goods. Obedience to this instruction doubtless irked the owners and shippers most,
and their vigorous protests moved the Holy Office to
instruct the agents to perform their functions with
great circumspection, carefully restoring the contents
of each inspected case to their original place.

The entire procedure seems ordinarily to have been
exceedingly perfunctory, with the questioning a hasty,
mechanical mumbling which fulfilled the letter rather
more than the spirit of the regulations. Even the directing heads of the Inquisition acknowledged that a full
compliance in writing "would be a lengthy and labo-
rious task for those in charge of it" and recommended
that the questions and answers be given orally; only
in the event that the cross-examination produced evidence of a serious infraction was a detailed record necessary. If there was nothing untoward the scribe made a
few notations of a summary character, which included
indications of the place of the *visita*, the port from
which the ship sailed, the date of arrival, the names of
the inspectors, the *maestre*, pilot, passengers or sailors
quizzed, and the gist of the information elicited. While
these data were jotted down the deputy had a few
cases opened and, after this cursory examination, he
stated that, so far as the Holy Office was concerned,
disembarkation of passengers and freight could proceed
at once. The completed report in its short, terse form
was then signed by the representative of the Inquisition, the shipmaster, the pilot, and the other witnesses
if they were able to write, and finally the whole was
countersigned by the notary.

When the inquiry brought unsatisfactory replies or suspicious findings a more extensive document was obligatory. But even where questionable literature was uncovered experience appears to have taught the Holy Office in Mexico City not to place too much reliance on the discretion of its own representatives at Vera Cruz. An edict of 1572 declared that if, on opening cases or boxes, *any* books of sacred writings, philosophy, or related subjects were noticed, the inspectors must promptly close the containers in question without attempting to read or even glance through such printed works. It was then their duty to place the seal of the Holy Office on the shipment and forward it directly to Mexico City for checking at the head office of the Inquisition before the owners could take possession. Even books consigned to other parts of the vast viceroyalty must be routed in the same way.

One other aspect of the Inquisition's instructions to its subordinates at Vera Cruz invites attention. The *visitas* in which they participated not uncommonly degenerated into more or less convivial meetings, with the shipmaster acting as host. Food was liberally dispensed and wine flowed freely. No doubt merchants on the incoming vessels contributed to these festivities for certain ulterior motives of their own. Where the fleet was large the necessity of visiting so many of its units must have been a severe test of the bibulous proclivities of the deputies and their assistants. Under these circumstances bargains and agreements of a private nature affecting the entry of books and other articles of possibly contraband character into the realm were doubtless consummated. Conceivably, the agents of the Holy Office were induced to *hacer la vista gorda*, as the Spaniards so expressively put it; that is, like their fellow inspectors of the Crown, they overlooked certain irregularities in the clearing of cargoes at the port. The stern and repeated admonitions of the chief Inquisitors to their deputies against accepting gratuities, gifts, or presents from anyone on the incoming ships amply confirm the existence of these abuses. Subordinates

were expressly forbidden at the time of the *visita* to
dicker or attempt to buy anything on shipboard—"not
even something to eat"—for themselves or for a third
party because, indeed, such an act would be "a bad example and *desedificación.*" Thus it is clear that the purposes of the inquisitorial inspection were often defeated
by flagrant flouting of its regulations, and by the connivance of the representatives of the Holy Office itself
with arriving passengers or crew.

Relations between the examiners and the examined
were sometimes badly strained, however. During the
1585 *visita* the commissioner of the Inquisition had
occasion to send for the shipmaster of *La Trinidad.*
When the messenger of the dread institution came
aboard to aprise its master of his errand, he found
that worthy in shirt sleeves and underdrawers engaged
in a friendly game of poker, or its equivalent. He was
playing for stakes of silk stockings at seven pesos a
pair and, as he had a hand or two more to play, this
crusty seaman refused to heed the summons at once
and growled that he would show up later in the afternoon. Pressed by the troubled messenger to come right
away as ordered, the exasperated *maestre* bellowed
loudly enough to be heard by everyone in the immediate vicinity, telling the inquisitorial emissary, with
particularly lurid epithets, to get out. Such a shocking
disregard of the expressed command of so august a
corporation as the Holy Office was an indignity not to
be tolerated, especially as this sort of thing was becoming distressingly common, and the offending shipmaster soon found himself clapped into jail and obliged to
put up a heavy bail to defray the expenses of trial. The
shortage of seamen in the port, however, was great
and there was a pressing need to prepare the fleet to
resume its voyage—facts which possibly explain in part
this mariner's independence and insolence. The ur-
gency of the naval situation at the moment was much
too severe to spare any member of the crews and, when
word of the shipmaster's plight reached the General
of the fleet an hour or so later, he hurried to plead

personally for the release of the culprit. The high authority and the indispensability of the shipmaster's services provided irresistible pressure, and the deputy of the Holy Office promptly acceded to the General's request. When the matter was reported later to the chief Inquisitor in Mexico City, that official wrote back that the commissioner had done entirely right in jailing the disrespectful skipper; instead of locking him up for only an hour, however, he should have done so for a week!

There were doubtless many similar clashes between the inspectors and the inspected, and numerous occasions when injured vanity, jealous resentment, and tactless acts on both sides caused friction and delay. Officious inquisitors, overconscious of their importance as guardians of the one True Faith, sometimes adopted an imperious manner at which equally individualistic shipmasters and pilots, accustomed to absolute command on their own vessels, did not fail to take umbrage. Well aware, too, of the manifest hypocrisy of these deputies, who were not averse to bribery in one form or another, both the crew and the passengers accorded them scant courtesy. As a consequence, arriving voyagers were sometimes subjected to petty annoyances by these pompous and too meticulous officials who searched their cabins and baggage for banned books and other contraband with excessive zeal. In 1575, for example, the deputy of the Holy Office and his assistants boarded the good ship *La Candelaria* where they found copies of prayer books and other devotional works, *Amadís*, and several other romances of chivalry, a *Life of St. Francis*, and also a *Life of Julius Caesar*, which had diverted some of the passengers during the crossing. The last-mentioned volume was in the possession of a student named San Clement, a somewhat indiscreet youth, apparently. On finding this book among the young man's personal effects the inquisitorial inspector felt called upon to emit a literary judgement on the youthful traveler's reading tastes. Departing from the ritualistic interrogations of the *visita* the official queried the student as to why he did not read something better, such as the life of St. Francis, who was a Christian? Why did he waste his time perusing a volume about Julius Caesar who had gone to hell, anyway, because, you know, that hero of ancient Rome was never baptized? This impertinent intrusion into the young scholar's reading preferences quite naturally irritated him and, not having reached full maturity, he was so injudicious as to engage in a heated argument with the censorious representative of the Inquisition. This unwise reaction to bureaucratic interference resulted in the drawing up of a judicial brief against him, in which this admirer of Julius Caesar was placed in the category of one suspect in the faith. How this rash youth emerged from his embarrassing predicament the existing records do not reveal. But the reiterated admonitions of the executive officers of the Holy Office in Mexico City to their subordinates in Vera Cruz and elsewhere to perform their duties with courtesy and tact indicate that incidents of this sort did not increase the popularity of the *visita*, and that secular complaints from influential sources were so numerous that even the powerful institution of the Inquisition could not ignore them. Such excess of zeal on the part of their employees was likely to be self-defeating, particularly when it operated in conjunction with other factors tending to foster resistance to vexatious restrictions.

Between the obvious unpopularity of the Inquisition's efforts to intervene in the commercial importation of books into the colonies and the prevalence of corruption among its own servitors, it is not surprising that the precautions and measures taken to prevent smuggling were largely ineffectual. Even if, as is so often alleged, the Holy Office had sought to exclude the romances of chivalry and other forms of light fiction—which it clearly did not do—some of these books, doubtless many, would have slipped through the barriers just as forbidden works actually did. The fact that superiors of the Inquisition issued edict after edict and command after command, demanding the utmost care and vigilance in the inspection of incoming vessels, offers convincing evidence that the attempt to suppress truly contraband literature, such as Lutheran tracts and Bibles, frequently failed. The smuggling of heretical works was continuous and even members of the religious communities themselves participated in this illegal traffic.

The choice of colonial book buyers in entertaining literature was as wide as that of their relatives in Spain itself. Depite the long delays caused by the slowness of the means of transportation and by the bureaucratic routines of the House of Trade and the Holy Office, the time lag in obtaining copies of the more recent literary successes of the Peninsula was remarkably short. Even if these agencies, particularly the Inquisition, had sought to keep the fiction works out of the hands of the overseas readers—and, of course, early royal decrees had endeavored to do just this—resourceful bookdealers would doubtless have found means to supply the lucrative demand. That they were often able to do so even with the clearly forbidden religious and theological writings is evident from the need of the Holy Office to make periodic rounds of the city shops in an effort to detect the source of contraband literature that continued to find its way into colonial hands. Now and then bookdealers were obliged to submit inventories of their stock to the authorities of the Inquisition, and now and then one found himself in serious difficulties with this censorious corporation which, in its self-imposed task of protecting the moral and spiritual welfare of the community, took upon itself the functions of municipal police. Its officers even resorted to raids on the bookstores under pressure from Spain or from local sources, but the intervals between these forays were usually long, during which the sale of printed works of all kinds proceeded quietly as a legitimate part of the commercial activity of colonial society.

The fiction, poetry, and drama of Spain's great writers stirred the hearts and minds of the Spanish-speaking peoples on both sides of the Atlantic throughout the centuries of imperial glory and national decline.

HUBERT HOWE BANCROFT

The Struggle Between
an Archbishop and a Viceroy
in Seventeenth-Century New Spain

Churchmen in no way involved with the Inquisition frequently clashed with civil administrative authorities in Spanish America. One example of this is found in the conflict that erupted in seventeenth-century New Spain between two iron-willed protagonists, one an archbishop, the other a viceroy. The story is told with great gusto in the Bancroft History of Mexico.

Born in 1823, Hubert Howe Bancroft became a successful San Francisco bookseller and eventually came to maintain agents in various parts of the world instructed to procure, by virtually any means, books and documents relating to the Spanish origins of the Pacific Coast region of the American Hemisphere, from the northern reaches nearly to the equator. Bringing together a large and generally anonymous work force, Bancroft published under his name a thirty-nine volume history of the Pacific Coast of the American Hemisphere, Alaska to Panama, among other works. Also included in the history was the southwestern region of the present United States.

Bancroft was anticlerical, and never missed an opportunity to make an interpretative analysis that cast churchmen in an unfavorable light. Nevertheless, his

From Hubert Howe Bancroft, *History of Mexico* (San Francisco, California, 1883), III, excerpts from pp. 33-78.

works have scarcely been excelled as a repository of factual material. His vast collection was acquired by the University of California in 1905, and constitutes the nucleus of the famous Bancroft Library.

PHILIP IV, convinced that reform was needed in New Spain, looked about for a man whose character and attainments should fit him for the task. Such a one soon presented himself in the person of Diego Carrillo de Mendoza y Pimental, second son of the marquis of Tavara, himself conde de Priego and marqués de Gelves.

At Mexico it had ever been a current saying that in keeping the friars and the Indians in order a viceroy had his hands full; Gelves accomplished more in a week than others in a month. But this very excess of zeal wrought his own undoing.

The course of the marquis of Gelves was commended by the upright, but these were far less in number than the vicious and the number of his enemies increased daily. Pedro de Vergara Gaviria, the senior *oidor*, was a self-willed man, who was not at all inclined to brook the restraint imposed upon him by the just though severe measures of the viceroy. Gelves, always courteous in his treatment of members of the *audiencia* and the *cabildo*, went further than necessary in useless attempts to make a friend of this man, who on his part seemed to consider all the favors of the marquis as so many marks of weakness.

By far the most formidable of the enemies of the marquis was the archbishop, Juan Pérez de la Serna. The zealous introduction of reforms by Gelves at first won the admiring cooperation of Serna, but when he found them extending too far within ecclesiastical precincts impatience turned into open hostility, for the prelate was exceedingly jealous concerning his prerogatives, and possessed of a stubbornness which readily developed into unreasonable zeal. He took in dudgeon the well-meant counsels concerning the reform of abuses in the ecclesiastical court, and on several occasions he forgot the dignity of his station, and that the viceroy was the personal representative of the king whom he served.

In September 1622, Manuel Soto, a person employed in the public granary of Mexico, denounced to the viceroy Melchor Pérez de Varáez, *alcalde* [mayor] of Metepec, accusing him of forcing the Indians of his jurisdiction to purchase grain of him at an exorbitant price, and to sell to him their cattle and produce at merely nominal rates, as well as other oppressive acts. The viceroy caused the charges to be investigated, and the proofs being irrefutable, ordered the less important to be made grounds of action in Mexico while the more grave he referred to the Council of the Indies. Meanwhile, Varáez had been under arrest in a private house, and Gelves ordered that, under bond, he should be given the freedom of the city. Varáez, fearing lest he might be again imprisoned, hastened to claim sanctuary at the convent of Santo Domingo.

Shortly afterward, Soto having alleged that Varáez contemplated fleeing to Spain, guards were placed at the door of his cell, and all communication with him was forbidden. He contrived, however, that a memorial should reach the archbishop, in which it was claimed that the presence of the guards was in violation of the right of sanctuary. The ecclesiastical judge ordered that the guards should be removed within two days, a demand to which the civil judges refused to accede.

The archbishop excommunicated Soto, the civil judges, the guards, and even the counsel employed by them. The persons so excommunicated immediately appealed to the audiencia.

A few days afterward Gelves called upon the archbishop to send the ecclesiastical judge to him that he might be purged of contempt [for countermanding the order of the civil tribunal that guards be posted about the Santo Domingo convent where Varáez had sought sanctuary]. After repeated instances the prelate reluctantly consented to do so. The ecclesiastical judge was found guilty of contumacy, and, being condemned to loss of property and banishment, he was taken to San Juan de Ulúa that he might be sent to Spain.

The archbishop immediately declared that the viceroy had incurred the censures mentioned in the bull called *In cœna Domini*. He therefore excommunicated him, ordering his name to be placed in the list of excommunicated persons affixed to the church door.

Gelves now called the oidores and the alcaldes of the audiencia together in order to get their opinion concerning the right of the archbishop to excommunicate him. Their answer was evasive, and he submitted the matter to a second assemblage, composed of ecclesiastics and laymen, who decided that the archbishop was clearly in the wrong. Fortified by this opinion the viceroy now retaliated on his antagonist by a decree condemning him to pay a fine of ten thousand ducados and confiscating his temporal property.

The archbishop resolved upon a last desperate resort. At an early hour on the 11th of January, 1624, he caused himself to be taken to the viceregal palace, in a sedan-chair borrowed for the purpose, and attended only by two pages. That he went in this ostentatiously humble manner, instead of in his coach, with crozier upborne before him and accompanied by the members of his household, was of itself a circumstance sufficiently strange to create attention, and on reaching the palace he was surrounded by a crowd of idlers.

The startled oidores asked what he desired. The prelate replied that he sought justice, and that he would not leave the audience-chamber until he had received it. He then desired to read a petition in which it was set forth: that he was obliged to appear thus in person because the president of the audiencia had given orders that no communication brought from him by an ecclesiastic would be received, and no layman dared to aid him in presenting one. Since it was not just that he alone in all New Spain should be denied the right to appeal to the audiencia for protection, he humbly besought that body, in the name of God and the church, to pity the wretched condition of the country, and also his dignity and jurisdiction, and to receive and hear without delay his petition against the threatened actions of the viceroy and, in addition, in regard to the matter of the guards of Varáez.

The prelate was now formally required to return to his palace, there to await the answer to his petitions, which must pass through the usual course. This he refused to do, insisting upon receiving justice and upon the admission of appeals. For this obstinacy he was fined four thousand ducados, and upon his further refusal the sentence of banishment from New Spain was added.

It was afternoon when Gelves ordered Lorenzo de Terrones, *alcalde del crimen* of the audiencia, to execute the sentence by taking the rebellious prelate to San Juan de Ulúa, there to embark for Spain. Accompanied by the *alguacil* mayor of Mexico City, Martín Ruiz de Zavala, his deputy, Baltasar de Parea, and others, Terrones notified the archbishop of the instructions he had received. The reply of the prelate was that they must remove him forcibly, and Terrones and Parea, taking him each by an arm, but in a respectful manner, led him down to the courtyard, where a hired travelling-carriage drawn by four mules was in waiting.

So great was the crowd in the plaza that with difficulty a passage was made. On all sides the sobs of the women mingled with the sterner voices of the men, while they asked whither their beloved pastor was being taken, or heaped imprecations on the head of the author of this outrage.

That night the three oidores, whether influenced by partisans of the archbishop or fearful that their action had been hasty, took counsel of one another. The result was that they despatched a messenger to Terrones bidding him go slowly, for on the morrow the order touching the exile of the prelate would undoubtedly be revoked. On the morning of the 12th, the oidores met again and passed another resolution [revoking their decision of the 11th and] ordering that the archbishop be brought back to Mexico. Informed of this meeting of the oidores, the viceroy ordered them into confinement within the palace. He also ordered that no action should be taken in the matter of the revocation by the oidores, in which he had had no part.

On the morning of the 13th Terrones entering the bed-chamber of the archbishop found him still abed. He desired the prelate to dress and to enter the carriage which was in waiting at the door. Informed of the action of the oidores, the archbishop pleaded that his health would not allow him to pursue the journey for the present. Terrones insisting, he replied curtly that a formal order would alone have weight with him. Not wishing to take extreme measures, Terrones sent to Mexico City for further orders. Alarm at his spiritual plight may have been one of the reasons why Terrones consented to humor the prelate, but for this he was reprimanded by the viceroy, who intimated that a little compulsion would do no harm.

The afflicted Terrones accordingly issued orders for departure. The luggage was sent on before, the carriage stood in readiness, but no archbishop appeared. At first the attendants of the prelate gave out that he was at his prayers, and then that he had gone for a walk; but, on more special inquiry, it was found that he was actually in the church of the Franciscan convent. Terrones followed him, accompanied by the local alguacil mayor, Torres, and four of the reluctant guard. On entering the church they found the prelate, in rochet, cape, and stole, standing by the high altar, while the *ciborium* was open with the host in monstrance within. When the alcalde desired him to leave and to continue the journey, the archbishop burst into tears, exclaiming that he had not wished to resort to this extremity in Mexico, for the land was newly christianized, and he feared lest the faith of the Indians might be shaken by the occurrence of events to them inexplicable. "Here, however," he added, "all are Spaniards; just as I am, take me away." Thus saying, he placed the paten upon the altar.

Terrones then ordered the notary to instruct the captain of the guard to do as the viceroy had ordered. As, in obedience to the thrice-repeated order, Armenteros and one of the guards began to ascend the steps of the altar, the archbishop arose, and lifting the paten on high before them he said: "Let us see if there is a Christian man so dead to shame as to lay hands on Jesus Christ" [in the Catholic faith, the host in monstrance, before which the prelate stood, is the actual Divine Lord, Jesus Christ]. The intangible power of the church was still paramount. Terrones took his wonted way out of his difficulties, and bade Torres ride with speed to Mexico City in order to give an account to the viceroy of the turn matters had taken. The latter merely replied that Terrones should be recalled and give place to a man who would carry out orders rather than write dispatches. All that night the prelate remained at the post he had chosen near the high alter, taking such rest as he could on its steps, regardless of the cold. All night the sacrament remained exposed on that altar while the guard kept watch by turns.

Among the oldest and most sacred spots of Anáhuac was Teotihuacan. During the early Nahua period its lofty pyramids were famed throughout the land. Here kings and priests were elected, ordained, and buried, and here were fulminated oracles which overturned dynasties and caused nations to tremble. It was in the village near this spot that Archbishop Serna had taken a defiant stand within the convent church, and like his ancient forerunners he sent forth a decree which should rouse a people and overturn a ruler. This was nothing less than a new excommunication of the viceroy, together with an interdict upon the whole capital.

They were faithful children, these poor Mexicans. They could not bear to see the representative of heaven driven forth like a criminal. To many it seemed an overwhelming calamity, and impressed by the popular disquietude others readily drifted into the current of excitement which at any moment might develop into a storm.

At eight o'clock on the morning of the 15th the great square of Mexico City was full of excited people. Armed with sharp fragments of stone gathered from the spot where the great cathedral was a-building, they soon forced the guard to retire within the palace gates, against which the mob, which had now assumed formidable proportions, threw itself. Presently the rioters began to cry that unless their pastor were restored to his flock they would put an end not only to all in the palace but to the tribunals and the gentry as well.

Warned by the insensate outcry against him, Gelves resolved [by evening] to seek safety in flight. He donned the garments of a servant, took off his well-known spectacles, and favored by the darkness he mingled with the mob, shouting awhile as lustily as any of them against himself. With two servants he thereupon hurried to San Francisco convent, and hid in a room behind the refectory.

Meanwhile the archbishop [having been contacted by representatives of the audiencia] set out [for Mexico City], escorted by a crowd, which greatly swelled as he advanced. At Guadalupe he was met by a procession of Indians with blazing torches, the advance guard of many others, and the entry into the capital about midnight resembled that of a victorious monarch. The houses were illuminated, the bells pealed merrily, and cheering crowds lined the street, impressed more than ever by the grandeur and power of the church. In the morning the prelate removed the interdict, and then, borne aloft to the altar over the heads of the crowds, he held mass and chanted the Te Deum, the rest of the day, a Tuesday, being held as a feast.

Notwithstanding the secrecy concerning his abode the viceroy had not failed from the first to let it be known that he was still among the living. On the very evening of his flight he had commissioned two men to treat with the audiencia for his restoration to power, and for a meeting between them. While considering themselves firmly enough established to follow their bent, the oidores nevertheless thought it necessary to call a meeting of leading men to give them support. Thus strengthened in their position, Gaviria and his colleagues replied to Gelves that he had been deposed not by them but by the people, and had virtually admitted the removal by abandoning his post. Under the circumstances the law and the popular will demanded that they should administer the government till the king decided in the matter.

Meanwhile, clergy, oidores, and local authorities of Mexico had combined to gather evidence against the viceroy, and in support of their acts, and this evidence together with exculpatory letters were forwarded by the fleet which set sail for Spain shortly after the riot.

The archbishop showed himself no less energetic in collecting and wording his evidence, in which he figured as a martyr to religion. The viceroy had interfered also in his jurisdiction, and had persecuted clergymen and oidores for daring to expostulate. In support of his representation he did not hesitate to include the declaration of aged nuns, who professed to have beheld the viceroy's adherents in the form of demons, and to have heard a supernatural voice denounce the marquis for his disobedience to the prelate. To another had been revealed that those who attacked the palace were souls from purgatory led by their guardian angel.

The court was not a little astonished and perplexed on receiving the news from Mexico. It could not decide with whom the blame should rest, although the defense of the archbishop appeared by no means satisfactory. One thing was certain however, that the authority of the king had been defied in his representative, and that an audiencia which had failed to support him at a critical moment could not be trusted with supreme control.

It was decided to appoint a new viceroy, one possessed of firmness to assume control of an apparently disordered country and with sagacity to guide an investigation and restore harmony by reconciling discordant elements, for it was not thought either prudent or needful to send troops. Such a man it was thought might be found in the governor of Galicia, Rodrigo Pacheco y Osorio, marqués de Cerralvo, who combined great physical strength with tried bravery. These qualities had however contributed less, it is said, to obtain the favor which he enjoyed at court than the fortunate circumstances that he once saved the queen by carrying her away from a fire. Cerralvo entered Mexico informally toward the end of October, 1624, conferred for some time with Gelves, and inquired into the state of affairs.

Archbishop Serna was among those who had hurried out of the way to Spain. The effect of his conduct in causing riot and overthrow of the royal representative must have startled him when sober second thought prevailed. His position became uncomfortable; he felt that he must personally plead his cause at court, and in the spring of 1624 he departed from Mexico. The desire to anticipate the disgrace of a recall may have been an additional motive. A prelate whose obstinacy had been the chief cause for bringing into contempt a royal representative, and into peril the authority of the crown, so as to require costly and radical measures, such a man could not expect a welcome. He was certainly treated coldly; but the Pope felt pleased with so firm a champion of the church, and recommended his cause to the king. Other influences were brought to bear; so that Serna was partially restored to favor and granted the important see of Zamora. He died in 1631, with the reputation of an able bishop and a benevolent man.

The monarch had good reason to be dissatisfied with the leading personages in this outbreak, with the viceroy for being so exacting and unyielding, and with the prelate for his excess of zeal, when, as one who professed to set an example of humility, he should have contented himself with a protest and appeal to the sovereign, especially in view of the insignificance of the point involved and the well-known temper of the marquis. The ecclesiastics, on whom the crown above all relied for supporting its authority, since troops were not kept, had been the chief promoters of the riot, wherein they proved themselves possessed of a greater power than that of the state.

MATHIAS C. KIEMEN

The Debate Over Indian Policy

in Seventeenth-Century Brazil:

The Jesuits vs. the Colonists

and Local Government Officials

In seventeenth-century Brazil, the most powerful representatives of the Catholic Church were the Jesuits. In their endeavors to protect the Indians against the alleged exploitation of the colonists and government officials, the Jesuits demanded virtually exclusive control over the natives. For a time, when they wielded vast influence at the Lisbon court, the Jesuits had their way. By 1661, however, the town councils in northern Brazil and other government bureaucrats took matters into their own hands and initiated a move that resulted in the temporary expulsion of the Jesuits. The Portuguese crown at this time passed into the hands of a king who did not sympathize with the Jesuits, and who upheld the actions of the colonists. Thus the conflict between churchmen and local lay officials ended in victory for the civil government of Brazil.

Rev. Mathias C. Kiemen, O.F.M., has in recent years served as editor of The Americas, a quarterly published by the Academy of American Franciscan History, and

From Mathias C. Kiemen, *The Indian Policy of Portugal in the Amazon Region, 1614-1693* (Washington, D.C., 1954), excerpts from pp. 79-117. Reprinted by permission of the Catholic University of America.

has conducted extensive research in colonial Brazilian history.

THE Jesuit effort on behalf of the Indians of Maranhão and Pará was intensified during the years 1652-1662 largely through activities of Father Antônio Vieira.

Antônio Vieira, whom many consider the most celebrated sacred orator in the Portuguese language, was born in Lisbon on February 6, 1608, of parents of moderate means. The family moved to Bahia when he was six years old. He attended the Jesuit College in Bahia, and in 1623 entered the Jesuit Order. In 1614 he returned to Portugal where he soon gained the confidence of King John IV. From 1652, when he was sent to Maranhão with royal authority to organize the Indian missions, until the day of his death in Bahia in 1697, he was intimately connected with the legislation passed in favor of the Indians.

On February 23, 1652, by decree of the king, Maranhão and Pará became separate captaincies, independent of each other. Each was now to have a *capitão-mor* who would exercise the highest civil authority. In accordance with the new law, Ignacio de Rego Barreto on March 3, 1652, was appointed for Pará, and Baltasar de Sousa Pereira on April 16, 1652, for Maranhão. Pereira arrived in São Luiz [the capital of Maranhão] in November or December of 1652, provided with a *regimento* which obliged him, among other things, to free the Indians who had been enslaved up to that time. Unfortunately for Vieira, Pereira published this part of his *regimento* only fifteen days after Vieira's arrival, and this led many of the people who were in favor of the *status quo* to blame the Jesuit for Pereira's action. A riot eventually broke out, during which people shouted, "Away with the Jesuits," but nothing more was accomplished. On March 2, 1653, the following Sunday, Vieira told the faithful from the pulpit that those who held slaves unjustly were on the road to eternal damnation.

On May 20 Fr. Antônio Vieira wrote a long letter

to the Portuguese monarch. He spoke of the miserable lot of the Indians, both free and slave, especially of those who lived with the Portuguese. The free Indians worked for the governors and captains, especially in the growing and curing of tobacco, and they treated them as though they were actually slaves. Many of them died under their heavy yoke. Under the circumstances, the governors and captains, Vieira believed, should be forbidden to grow tobacco or any other product, or from using or distributing Indians in any way, except for public projects, such as the building of fortifications. Nor should they be permitted to place the *aldeias* [Indian communities] in the hands of laymen. On the contrary, no white man should be allowed in the *aldeias* except the missionary who lived there.

While Vieira was thus trying to influence the Crown, the settlers of the two captaincies were alert to the threat to the *status quo*. They therefore sent delegates (*procuradores*) to plead their case and obtain legislation favorable to their interests. The case, as presented by Vieira and the procurators, was resolved in Lisbon by the law of October 17, 1653, an attempt at a compromise solution.

Under given circumstances, the king allowed Indians to be captured as slaves. *Entradas* [entries into unpacified Indian territory] were permitted, with the choice of leader up to the captain or governor, in conference with the members of the town council, and the prelates of religious orders and the vicar general. Religious must accompany these expeditions, and the decision as to the legality of enslavement was up to this accompanying religious. The last part of the law absolutely forbade to the governor or captain-major the use of Indians in any way at all, except for public causes, such as building fortifications.

Such was the law of October 17, 1653. It was not entirely pleasing to Vieira, and he left for Lisbon in 1654, hoping to be able to improve it.

[Prior to leaving for Spain,] Vieira told the king quite specifically what should be done for the missions and the Indians in his letter of April 16, 1654. He outlined his ideas in nineteen paragraphs. [In the last of these Vieira insisted that the king] should place the missions in the hands of a single Order. Not every Order, in his opinion, would do. The work should be entrusted to an Order known for the virtue, disinterestedness, zeal and learning of its members. Moreover, the Indians should be independent of the authority of the governor.

Vieira left São Luiz in June, 1654, and arrived in Lisbon after a perilous voyage in November of the same year. There was much for him to do. The two procurators of the Town Councils of Belém [the capital of Pará] and São Luiz were already active at Court, protecting the interests of the colonists. The new governor of Maranhão-Pará [the two captaincies were now joined together under the rule of one governor] André de Vidal Negreiros, appointed on August 11, 1654, was ready to depart for his post. The king, however, anxious to settle this Indian question once for all, called a full-dress junta of the most prominent theologians in the country to decide the thorny question of Indian enslavement. The king first of all sent out, on March 15, 1655, copies of the older laws on the subject to a group of theologians, asking them for their opinions on the matter.

After giving the theologians time to form their opinions the king ordered the junta to meet, probably in early April. The meeting was presided over by the Archbishop of Braga, Dom Pedro de Alemcastre. Coincidental with this meeting, a similar meeting was held to discuss practical details. It was attended by the new governor, Fr. Vieira himself, and the two procurators.

The result of the deliberations of these two juntas was the law of April 9, 1655, which regulated Indian enslavement. The body of the law began with a prohibition against capturing Indians except in the cases to be enumerated. The first is in a just offensive war against the Indians, which is defined as a war fought with the written authority of the king, after he had asked the opinion of all the civil and religious officials in the state. This effectively took away the power to wage offensive war from the governor. The second case in which the Indians could be captured as slaves would be one in which they impeded the preaching of the Holy Gospel, for they were obliged to allow it to be preached to them, even though they could not be forced with arms to accept it and believe it. The third case would be if the Indians were ransomed while being *presos a corda para serem comidos* [prisoners who were to be eaten by their Indian captors]. The fourth case in which Indians could be legally enslaved would be if they were purchased from other Indians, whose legitimate slaves they were, having been taken in a just war of the Indians among themselves.

[In] the next section of the law the king forbade all governors to work tobacco, or to use or distribute the Indians in any way at all, nor could the governor place lay captains in the *aldeias*, since these villages were to be ruled by their pastors and the Indian chiefs.

It can easily be seen that the law of April 9 was concerned with only one facet of the Indian problem. It was supplemented in many practical details by the *regimento* given to André Vidal de Negreiros on April 14, 1655. The Indians were to serve six months of each year, divided into terms of two months at a time, after which they must spend two months at home. The payment for the two-month service must be made before the Indians left for the work. The *regimento* decreed concerning *entradas* that on the years when these were undertaken, the Indians of service would serve proportionately less time in working for the colonists. *Entradas* were to be made only for the purpose of the propagation of the Faith. The Prelate of the Missions would give the order for the *entrada*, and the governor was commanded to furnish him with the soldiers necessary and a suitable leader, who, however, should have nothing to do with the religious side of the expedition, only caring for the military preparations. The Jesuit prelate shall decide the time and place of the *entradas*.

These two documents of 1655, together with the inevitable appointment of Fr. Vieira as Superior of the Missions, were to be the foundations upon which the Jesuits attempted to build control of the Indians. Vieira left Lisbon on April 16. When he arrived in São Luiz, Negreiros was already there. Largely because of the governor's interest, the law and the *regimento* were immediately put into practice. The choice of governor had been a wise one. Negreiros knew the country well, being a Brazilian by birth. He was, moreover, openly in favor of missionary activities. The discontent of the colonists at the arrival of Negreiros and Vieira with such a strong law was general. It was hard for the settlers to realize that the Indians, the great source of wealth in the colony, were now completely entrusted to the Jesuits. Yet they had no alternative. The presence and prestige of Negreiros were sufficient to ensure the carrying out of the royal will in both Maranhão and Pará.

The colonists, however, were not all resigned to the new situation. Open trouble began in 1656. In Belém and São Luiz the residents suffered in silence, because of the closeness of the seat of government. But in Gurupá, many leagues from Belém, the settlers decided to take matters into their own hands. With the support of the soldiers of the fort, the colonists put the two local Jesuits in a canoe, took them to a spot near Belém and warned them not to return. The colonists did not know the temper of Governor Negreiros. Accompanied by thirty soldiers and sixty Indians, he immediately restored the Jesuits to their former position. Two of the guilty were sent in chains to Lisbon to be judged there. The other lesser culprits were exiled to Brazil. Clearly the new governor was not to be trifled with. For the time being, at any rate, Vieira could congratulate himself on the victory.

But *requerimentos* continued to be sent to Lisbon against the law. The complaints of the colonists, however, would be useless as long as Father Vieira kept his influence at Court and could count on the protection of the royal family.

Early in 1661 the troubles of the Jesuits with the colonists and government officials reached a critical stage. Repeated complaints of the people to the Jesuits in Maranhão and Pará in 1659 and 1660 had had no effect. On January 12, 1660, the Town Council of Belém had written to the officials of São Luiz, suggesting a united front of complaints against the Jesuits' temporal power. But São Luiz turned down this proposal. One last series of appeals was made in 1661 by the Town Council of Belém to Fr. Vieira. On January 15, the town council in a long reclamation, declared the utter helplessness of the colony without more Indian workers. The town council then resolved to send a procurator to see the governor in São Luiz to tell him about conditions, and also to send a supplication to the Court. The complaint to the Court was sent off on April 9. So far all the agitation had been in Belém. The scene now shifted to São Luiz, where some private letters of Fr. Vieira to the bishop who had been confessor of the king were made public in early 1661. These letters were full of complaints against the lawlessness of the people concerning the protective legislation for the Indians. On May 17 the procurator or commissary sent by the Town Council of Belém left that city on his way to São Luiz. His arrival in São Luiz and the story he told, together with the publication of the recent letters, was enough to cause a riot in São Luiz, which ended in the imprisonment within the college of all Jesuits. That the revolt succeeded was due in part to the indecisiveness of the governor, Pedro de Melo [Negreiros had returned to Portugal after serving only eighteen months as governor], when the fatal moment of the revolt arrived. It must be said, however, that his military guards deserted him at the crucial moment. In a letter to Fr.

Vieira which the governor sent off on May 23, he asked Vieira what he could have done with five or six faithful soldiers against five or six hundred rioters.

Vieira was sailing from Belém in Pará and stopped midway at the captaincy of Cumá, where the letter of the governor reached him. He immediately returned to Belém, where, he trusted, the news had not yet arrived, and where he could possibly still save the situation. He arrived in Belém on June 21 and immediately addressed himself to the town council, urging them to repudiate the actions of São Luiz. On July 7 the emmissary that had been sent by Belém to the governor some time before returned to Belém and made his report. The governor had granted part of their request: that the Jesuits be removed from their temporal control over the Indians. When news of the happenings in Maranhão spread through the city, the excitement grew. On July 17 a tumult arose among the people, who demanded the immediate election of a *juiz do povo* to settle the Indian question. The town council elected Diogo Pinto, one of their number, to this position, and the tumult died down. The new judge immediately imprisoned Vieira and his companions and sent them to São Luiz. From there the fathers were sent to Lisbon on the first available ship. By the following year, 1622, all the fathers, even those in the faraway missions, had been rounded up and put into custody. The revolt was complete.

In Lisbon, Vieira immediately set about repairing the situation, and was having marked success, when, unexpectedly, on June 21, 1662, a palace revolution unseated the queen regent, Luisa. Her son, Alfonso VI, became king in fact as well as name. Unfortunately for his cause, Fr. Vieira had backed the losing faction which had supported Prince Pedro against his brother the king. Alfonso now turned on Vieira. The Jesuit was banished from Court, and, in fact, was in the toils of the Inquisition from 1663 to 1667. He returned to royal favor in 1668, when Pedro became regent, but he never regained his former pre-eminence. In 1669 he went to Rome, and there he stayed until 1679. After that he went to Bahia, where he spent his declining years until his death in 1697.

· II ·

THE

First Century

OF Independence

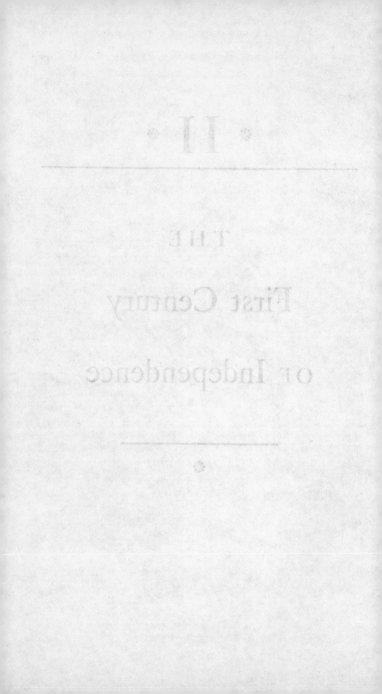

AURELIO ESPINOSA POLIT

Catholicism and
the National Tradition

In 1896 an anticlerical, liberal movement triumphed in Ecuador. Its leaders set about to revoke the imposing privileges that Gabriel García Moreno had conferred upon the Church during the 1860-1875 period. One effect of the ensuing liberal legislation was to remove religious instruction from the public schools and to make it extremely difficult for the Church to operate private schools. Aurelio Espinosa Polit, born in Quito in 1894, grew up during the period of liberal ascendancy. Ordained a Jesuit priest after advanced studies in Belgium and Spain, he campaigned tirelessly to free private education in Ecuador from government interference. In 1944 he was instrumental in obtaining an educational reform that granted considerable autonomy to private schools. The following year he was appointed Rector of the Catholic University of Ecuador. Like so many Catholics throughout Latin America, Espinosa Polit continued steadfastly to voice the sentiments of García Moreno: the Catholic faith has been the principal creative factor in molding the national character, and there can be no national unity unless the traditional influence of the Church is maintained.

FATHERLAND! Who does not thrill to its mystic appeal? Who does not feel himself a part of its very

From Aurelio Espinosa Polit, *Temas Ecuatorianos* (Quito, 1954), excerpts from pp. 279-290. By permission of the Instituto Superior de Humanidades Clásicas, Quito, Ecuador.

essence, joined to it by every fiber of his being? Yet, very few if any can set forth with philosophical precision the elements that constitute the Fatherland. In fact, it may be impossible to capture in a definition the essence of the Fatherland. Although we cannot define it, we can intuit perfectly and clearly what it is. And because of this we love the Fatherland above all other mundane realities, and we are ready to sacrifice even our lives for it.

Territory, people, nation, state: all these are elements that contribute to the concept of the Fatherland. But there is something more. Talk as we may about the land and about the blood of which we are so proud, about the nationality we claim as our own and about the government that rules us, we have still not come close to touching upon all that we understand by the word Fatherland. In addition to all those elements that are visible and tangible, we realize that there is something else which constitutes the Fatherland, something that we may call the "informing spirit," something that becomes an essential part of each and every one of the children of the Fatherland, something that gives meaning and life to the love they feel for it and inspires them to accept gladly all of the sacrifices that this love may demand from them.

Only one word can be used to describe this "something": it is tradition. Tradition is the soul of genuine patriotism. It is the rich common patrimony formed of the ideas and feelings of the populace; formed of the joys and sorrows, the failures and triumphs and all of the personal contributions of national geniuses, heroes, and saints. It is every vestige of civic virtue that can be transmitted to the future heirs of the nation. It is the vibrations of the national spirit shared by all generations, after a long and complex historical process that has forged the national spirit into a body of clear and distinct ideals.

Even this imposing enumeration of the attributes of tradition concerns only the outward elements that comprise it. A live, pulsating, and guiding tradition supposes two more factors: the deep, incontrovertible conviction, universally rooted in the people, of the immeasurable good that a common, inward, and spiritual patrimony provides for them; and, as a consequence of this conviction, the inflexible, universal will of protecting this patrimony, of strengthening and defending it, of making it imperishable.

Let us look at ourselves and inquire: do the Ecuadoran people have their own tradition? The answer is yes! They have a tradition of outward splendor. But do they have an inward, spiritual tradition of which they can be conscious, a deeply-rooted tradition shared by all, one whose essential integrity they are ready to defend? Yes, without any hesitation we answer yes. The universality of this categorical affirmation might be qualified by the concrete reality of the actual situation; but, we know that the only sensible approach is to consider the feelings of the majority. In dealing with vast collectivities in which each individual enjoys freedom of the will and liberty to reach his own judgements, an absolute unanimity of opinion is never possible.

A majority, an immense majority of the Ecuadoran people, shares and believes in the bountiful and genuine national tradition. I refer to a tradition that has emerged in the Ecuadoran nation, that has taken root in the agitated course of its secular history, that during many generations has been sifted and approved by the popular will, and ultimately assimilated as a part of the national consciousness. This is the only sort of tradition that can rightly be called national, because it is not the exclusive property or heritage of a political party; nor is it an importation from abroad. Only a tradition such as this can offer an accurate portrayal of the physiognomy of the Fatherland.

The basic element of the Ecuadoran tradition is Religion. On what page of the annals of our country is there not something to be said about Religion? From the very first moment, when the epic adventure of the conquest begins, the priest appears together with the soldier. The Dominicans who accompanied Francisco Pizarro were the first to step upon the Ecuadoran shore. The Franciscans and the Mercedarians accompanied Pedro de Alvarado to Ecuador, and the Mercedarians were also with Belalcázar. A secular priest, Bartolomé Segovia, came with Diego de Almagro to this land. Everywhere the priest, as a minister of the God of Peace, restrained and tempered the conqueror, poured the oil of mercy on the wounds left open by the warlike invasion, and brought conciliation between the mighty vanquisher and the defeated race. The priest, as the herald of joyous tidings, approached the Indian with love, and the happiness found in the newly acquired faith compensated for the Indian's loss of liberty. The priest, by bringing to America the light and regeneration of the faith, rendered Spain's rights of conquest legitimate, for it was only the evangelizing mission of the Spanish crown that conferred upon it the just right to rule the Indies.

The city of Quito, first germ of the future Ecuadoran nation, was founded on December 6, 1534. Among its first residents we find two priests, Juan Rodríguez and Francisco Jiménez, who at the little hermitage of Vera Cruz, and later at the first established parochial church, began to care for the spiritual life of the new-born city.

With the organization of civil institutions and the beginning of secular activity in Quito, Fray Jodoco appeared. Around this figure of glorious legend there gathered the brothers of the Seraphic Order, men who guided the souls of the Indians, who won the natives to the faith through religious instruction, who taught them to live in peace with the conqueror, and to cultivate all of the arts and to acquire the European civilization.

When the initial steps toward establishing a society had been taken and it was possible to commence the systematic work of providing for civilization and culture by means of public education, it was again the Church, and only the Church, which concerned itself with the monumental task. The unimpeachable words of history proclaim that during the entire period of the formation of the Ecuadoran nationality, our country had no other teacher than the Church. Only late, very late, did the state begin to play a role in public education. The high level of achievement that public education had attained with the cultural development of our country, and even the supreme importance that nowadays we attach to education, attest to the immense debt of gratitude that the Ecuadoran nation owes to the Catholic Church, which for centuries was its only teacher and counsellor. The first primary school, the first high school, the first university, were all exclusively the results of Church effort. Free of charge, the Church provided for the education of all social groups, the lowest as well as the highest. All of the religious orders contributed to this work of education, without which the Old Kingdom of Quito would have been a country of illiterates.

During the conquest and during the colonization period, the Church took the first steps toward providing for the organic life of the country, and toward developing a national culture. In order not to extend indefinitely the proofs of the universal influence of the Church in the life of our country, let us add just one more chapter, one that pertains to the role of the Church in the Ecuadoran independence movement. The Church effectively prepared the way for the wars of independence. It could not have been otherwise, for the complex and far-reaching effects of Church influence upon the entire Ecuadoran society had molded the historic personality in all of its aspects.

What a vast influence upon our legal habits and attitudes was exercised by the episcopal constitutions framed by the two great bishops of our early times, Fray Pedro de la Peña and Fray Luis López de Solís. The legal traditions which they established contributed to the making of the national personality that would one day discover it could continue its development only by throwing off the colonial bonds. How great also was the contribution of the popular religious devotions, uniquely our own, toward creating a unified spiritual basis for the hopes and aspirations of the whole people. The result of this contribution was that Ecuadorans became accustomed to Ecuadoran habits and usages. There was also the influence of our own religious art, an art inferior to none. This art led to the accomplishment of architectural wonders in the building of our convents; it led to exuberance within the limits of good taste in the decoration of our baroque temples; it produced exquisite delicateness in oil paintings and emotional vitality in polychrome carvings. This was an indigenous, original art that served as an interpreter of the national soul. Because it was everywhere, even in the households of the most humble families, this art contributed a sense of cultural and spiritual independence and originality to the national consciousness. This was a necessary background and prelude to the desire for political independence.

And when the moment came, the Church assisted the liberating movement, protecting it with her authority and directing it with her spirit. A clear proof of this is that at the very inception of the independence movement, there appeared the immortal motto: *Salva Cruce Liber Esto*. Liberty, yes! But at the same time, protection for religion, protection for the redeeming cross! A country of our own, but with the traditional religion, under the protection of the eternal cross!

It is impossible to study the history of our independence without discovering that the clergy were everywhere involved in it. Still more impossible is it to understand the national spirit without recognizing that this spirit is the product of the intimate union between Religion and Nation.

The conclusion following from this survey of our nation's history is inescapable. A vast multiplicity of different facts and divergent aspects of our historical development all unite to proclaim that, for the Ecuadoran, Religion and Nation are inseparable.

We must repeat: territory, people, nation, state, are

not enough to constitute the Fatherland. These material elements must be animated by a guiding, spiritual element which we call tradition: a tradition that has been assimilated by the national consciousness, that is rooted in the hearts of the people who sense it, who love it, and who are willing to defend it as their greatest treasure. Never can we hope sufficiently to emphasize how transcendent and how irreplacable a factor of our tradition is this spiritual element.

Do not wrest tradition from the people, do not mutilate or adulterate it lest you kill it! People without tradition do not comprise a Fatherland. They are a conglomerate group, without consistency, always in jeopardy of being victimized by the next national convulsion.

The tradition of the Ecuadoran people, as we have abundantly proved, is one in which religion is an essential element. Our tradition will be mutilated, and will in fact become false in its very essence, if we separate from it the animating religious spirit. It will be a tradition without the strength and virtue to achieve the union of our hearts if we dispense with the only factor that is capable of uniting our spirits, that is, the unifying strength of faith.

This is our historic reality. No subterfuge or sophistry can modify it. Under the protection of religion, our country has been fashioned. Thus was she born, thus did she grow up, thus did she become strong, thus did she attain the maturity of independent life, and thus, despite tragic aberrations, does she continue to exist.

It is said that the unanimity of our national spirit, based upon the intimate union of Religion and Nation, no longer exists. This is true. The unnatural sectarianism of our predecessors has destroyed this union. Entire sectors among the intelligentsia of the country have repudiated it. Ignoring its might as the most effective element of national cohesiveness, the civil authority has severed the ties between Religion and Nation, using as its sword the official doctrine of laicism. The sublime, pristine unity of our tradition has been shattered. Our tradition is now a cracked building. But the foundation endures, and it is sound.

We still place our confidence in this immovable foundation, despite the undeniable cracks in the edifice. A building with its foundation still intact can be repaired even when its structure has been grievously damaged. If need be, it can be rebuilt. This must be our work, and there is still time to accomplish it. With renewed energy, animated by the consciousness of our patriotic responsibilities, aware that whatever we do for religion we do for our country, we must struggle with mounting courage to preserve what is left of our religious treasure. We must strive to recover what has been lost. Nowadays, also, we must work toward rejecting the Protestant heresy that is trying to establish itself in our land.

WILLIAM REX CRAWFORD

Intellectual Opposition to

the Tradition of Catholicism

Many nineteenth-century Latin American intellectuals
questioned the value of colonial traditions, especially
of Catholicism. Strongly influenced by rationalism and
positivism, these men felt that colonial customs and
value judgements rendered Latin Americans peculiarly
ill prepared for achieving national economic maturity
and developing democratic institutions. Three intellectuals of these persuasions were the Chileans José
Victorino Lastarria and Francisco Bilbao, and the Peruvian Manuel González Prada. By judicious selections
from the writings of these men and by his own penetrating comments, William Rex Crawford gives a valuable
insight into the intellectual attitudes that underlay
much of Latin America's anticlericalism in the first
century of independence. Crawford has conducted extensive research in Latin America, and served as cultural attaché in Brazil, 1943-1945. He began his teaching career at the University of Pennsylvania in 1919,
and was director of that University's Institute of Hu-
manistic Studies for Executives from 1954 to 1960.

CHILE has perhaps not been sufficiently grateful to
Lastarria [1817-1888]. The boldness of his opinions

Reprinted by permission of the publishers and the author, from
William Rex Crawford, *A Century of Latin American Thought*,
Cambridge, Mass.: Harvard University Press, copyright 1945
and 1961, by the President and Fellows of Harvard College.
(Excerpts from pp. 57-64, 174-182.)

was not designed to conciliate, and the inflexible dog-
matism with which he imposed himself and his opinions did not please. He was, however, not only the
doctrinaire exponent of rationalism and positivism,
but a thinker who cared deeply for the welfare of his
country and sought to trace back the causes of its
problems to their roots.

A poor provincial boy from the down-at-the-heel
town of Rancagua, a few miles south of Santiago, José
Victorino Lastarria came to the capital to study during
the restless times of Portales' conservative dictatorship. The lack of liberty in the atmosphere seems to
have made the word ring in his mind ceaselessly. He
read, as we who take freedom for granted do not, the
classics that told the story of liberty and how to continue it: Comte, Rousseau, Montesquieu, Bentham.

The year 1843 was an important year in his life. In
June the first number of his fighting journal *El Cre-
púsculo* ("The Twilight") appeared; the following
month he entered Congress; and the new University
counted him among its professors in the Faculty of
Humanities. The Rector's address did not please him
too much, in spite of its "liberty in all things." There
was not enough demolition of the errors of the past
in it. He wanted to find the ideas that had made history what it was; [Andrés] Bello [a Venezuelan-born
intellectual who was a principal founder of educational
and legal institutions in Chile, and a friend and teacher
of Lasterria] was afraid of anything but facts and dis-
trusted the element of subjective interpretation to
which Lastarria would open the door. But it was Bello
himself who dryly gave him his chance, asking him to
prepare the address on the occasion of the first anniversary of the University. This address was a bombshell,
"Investigations on the Social Influence of the Conquest and the Colonial System of the Spaniards in
Chile" (1844).

"The Investigations" is a short book but it must have
been a very long speech. It proposes to use history as

a previous deposit of experience from which men can extract lessons that will save them from disaster and light that will guide them in the darkness of the future. Concretely, Lastarria asks, "What is the history of our republic? What profit can be drawn from its study for the direction of our affairs in their present condition?" and he answers, "The history of Chile is still that of a new people who can look back upon three centuries of a gloomy existence without movement."

All, he maintained, that can be said by the apologists of the colonial order to prove the virtue that flourished under that régime can be summed up in the statement that Chileans were docile followers of the religion they had been taught. Religion among them had been made the instrument of despotism instead of the basis of civilization and freedom, the highest guarantee of the rights of man. We must recognize in addition, he continued, that the Spanish régime left a heritage of conditions and even of character which constituted a great handicap to a people who would be free and progressive. The struggle between the past and the present goes on. "It is for us to study our own peoples, to come to know their errors and their problems, and thus appreciate the obstacles which stand in the way of their greater perfection and happiness . . . and destroy completely the resistance offered by the old Spanish system embodied in our society."

His examination of the social institutions of his own time reveals the fact that the Catholic Church has not been bound by those principles which he considers essential. It has, on the contrary, erected into religious dogmas all its aversions to the moral conquest of modern philosophy, and finds itself opposing the social and political rights which modern civilization demands for its members. The result is an irresistible movement toward the separation of church and state. As a part of this movement, he maintains, education will be taken away from the church and it will become a positivistic and scientific education without ceasing to inculcate the knowledge, love, and practice of what is just and true, making the good and useful citizen.

*　*　*　*　*

Lastarria was a valiant fighter for freedom, but he seems almost stodgy compared with the fiery [Francisco] Bilbao [1823-1865]. Lastarria's rejection of Spanish civilization was vigorous enough, but he retained Christianity. It was Bilbao's contribution—and it soon got him into hot water—that he could not separate Spanish civilization from Catholicism. The famous essay on "The Nature of Chilean Society" was published in June of 1844. It reminds one of the *Communist Manifesto* of the year before.

"Our past is Spain," he wrote. "Spain is the Middle Ages. The soul and body of the Middle Ages were Catholicism and feudalism." The faith was an instrument that the church used in its relations with the barbarians. It tried to subject everyone to its sway. Where there is no doubt that the coming of Christianity marked the greatest step forward in religious history, Catholicism was a reaction which deformed the primitive purity of the doctrine of Jesus. Its effects on women, children, citizens, and intelligentsia are analyzed by Bilbao: "The wife is subject to the husband. Slavery of the wife. . . . The child is irremediably subjected to the father. Slavery of the child. . . . The individual subjected to authority. Slavery of the citizen. . . . Thought chained to text, intelligence bound to dogma. Slavery of thought."

When we examine America, he continues, we see that it falls into two divisions: the English United States, and the Spanish Disunited States:

In the United States we see all the elements of their history united in a move toward greater and greater liberty. In the Disunited States we see the impotent efforts of Liberty, falling and rising again, always threatened, never secure, living through all the vicissitudes of a terrible alternation between despotism and attempts at freedom.

For this striking contrast, Bilbao can find no other valid explanation than the difference of religion between the two continents.

What has been the role of Catholicism in this continent of South America? he asks. To exterminate, to brand as heretics those who thought freely. To strive to keep in slavery a world that had won its political independence; to impose itself as a state religion, banish liberty of conscience, hinder immigration, lay an economic burden on the people, oppose all reform and progress, arouse the baser instincts of the multitude, fight reason, personality, sovereignty, and the principle of nationality.

"The American Gospel," published in 1864, is the same gospel he had been preaching since his twenties. It is still needed, he maintains, for America has no American Bible or Koran. He aspires to write it. Readers of his other books, he continues, hardly need to be told that Spain conquered America, the English the northern continent, and that the result of their divergent policies has been that the United States takes first place among nations old and new, while for the Disunited States progress consists in the task of "un-Spanishing" themselves. For Spain and Spanish history can be epitomized in a word, and that word is Catholicism. The liberty to think for oneself, which Spain proscribed, is a thread that runs through the origins and subsequent history of the United States. He even dares to use the word Protestant, and admits the close relation between the liberty of North America and the form its Christianity took. There have been few South Americans who would go this far; nearly all have been Catholic enough to be very sure they were not Protestants. He admits again, as few Latin Americans have done, that the United States is more than a rich or progressive nation; "it is the creative nation"; and he lists the glories of its thought and literature.

To be sure, he says, rationalism is even better than Protestantism; the smell of theology and of biblical learning clings to Protestantism, and leads to a perfect fury of interpretation and discussion which cannot be settled by the immediate appeal to reason that he would use. There is still revelation in the Protestant view of the universe; it is the best attitude that has been adopted by any historic society, but it is not the best possible attitude.

*   *   *   *   *

[Manuel] González Prada [1848-1918] stands out as Peru's most distinguished writer, although his qualities are most un-Peruvian, and his countrymen who preferred to be amused gave first place to Ricardo Palma, the author of the many volumes of charming *Tradiciones*. No later figure can rival don Manuel.

In 1887 González Prada married Adriana de Vereuil. He was almost forty and had done nothing he had planned; she animated him to return to the struggle.

It was a struggle. The articles of this period are called "Propaganda and Attack"; the great speech shouts, "Old men to the tomb, young men to work!" The question that agitated him was, under present circumstances, what are the duties of a Peruvian writer? He answered his own question by attacks on the church which pained his sisters and mother, who typically remained devout Catholics, and by ventilating the Indian question. "We are accomplishing the miracle of killing in the Indian something that dies hard in man, I mean hope."

An attempt to make a public speech on free thought led to government prohibition and student and worker support. An attempt at a radical journal, *Germinal*, taking the side of the people and attacking the clergy, led to its closing and the inauguration of a substitute, *The Independent*. The article "Politics and Religion" argues, in the face of a president who personifies clericalism, that liberty and Catholicism cannot exist side by side. Burned in effigy, attacked in the pulpit, González Prada continued the fight in the renewed *Germinal*, and moved closer to the working class, seeing in their support the only hope. The social question occupied him more and more, and the poet wrote an article against poetry that is mere entertainment.

Putting his truth before everything, he incurred the serious anger of his sister Isabel by a speech on "Women, the Church's Slaves." In politics he continued to lash out at the pseudo-democracy of Peruvian public life, and in literature to insist that poetry be judged by its social and political aims and results. Forsaking his own social class, he proclaimed his discovery that the proletariat would solve the social question in the only way possible, by revolution; the wind of rebellion, which came from solitary thinkers, as always, was beginning to stir the masses.

Anticlericalism is something that North America knows very little about, for the happy reason that it knows very little about what causes it. And so some of González Prada's paragraphs will seem crude and sensational.

What the priest does to children is even more pernicious than what he does to women. . . . We see the effect of religious education all the time, we feel it constantly. All those perverse, crooked souls, all those dry, selfish hearts, all those men who with one hand cross themselves while they stick the other in their neighbor's pocket, show plainly enough where they come from, they bear the stamp of religious education. With very rare exceptions, from time immemorial, priests have been the more determined oppressors of Humanity, especially of the underprivileged classes. In the past, they did nothing to abolish pauperism and improve the social conditions of the masses; in the present it is the same old story. . . . They perpetuate the grossest superstitions and live petrified in an atmosphere of errors and lies. They constitute a force hostile to civilization. . . . They have no reason to exist. Catholicism in this country has not gone a step beyond idolatry. Properly speaking, we do not have religion, but only religious practices. From the depths of the peoples to the surface of the ruling class, we find no men animated by a spiritual belief, but rabbles sunk in the grossest superstitions. . . . Our Catholicism is clericalism; worse still, it is rule by the friars.

The reader can turn to the prose of González Prada and find much more of the same kind of thing. It is easy to criticize, but does not much credit belong to a literary man who pinned his hopes on science, to an aristocrat who learned to look forward to the proletarian revolution, to the Spaniard of old family who gave the Indian first place among his country's problems, to the poet who accepted economics?

EMILIO PORTES GIL

The Conflict in Mexico Between

the Civil Power and the Clergy,

1854-1876: Defense of

the Civil Power

In 1854 a revolution destined to produce far-reaching consequences erupted in Mexico. The movement, begun primarily by guerrilla bands in the southern mountains under the leadership of Juan Álvarez, originally aimed at little more than the overthrow of President Antonio López de Santa Anna. Soon the revolution evolved into a movement aimed at ending the lingering influence of many colonial traditions and at creating a more representative governmental structure based upon the concepts of political and economic individualism. As it gained momentum, the revolution ushered in the period of The Reform (La Reforma) and gave rise to much anticlerical legislation, the value and consequences of which are still warmly debated. Emilio Portes Gil, born in 1891, served as provisional president of Mexico, 1928-1930. At the time of publication of his spirited defense of The Reform's anticlerical legislation, he was serving as Mexico's Secretary of Foreign Relations. The style of the English translation of the Portes Gil treatise, published in Mexico, leaves much to be

From Emilio Portes Gil, *The Conflict Between the Civil Power and the Clergy* (México, D.F., 1935), excerpts from pp. 61-80. By permission of the author.

desired. At least it preserves the heatedly partisan
character of the prose.

ON September 24, 1855, Juan Álvarez arrived at
Iguala, where he convened a national junta that was
to meet on October 4 in the city of Cuernavaca, in
order to appoint a provisional president pursuant to
the Plan of Ayutla [the Plan announced by the leaders
of the 1854 revolution, calling for the ouster of President Santa Anna and the convening of a constituent
congress]. Said junta appointed General Álvarez himself, and he in that capacity called an extraordinary
congress to constitute the nation under the form of a
democratic and representative republic.

Once President Álvarez had appointed all the members of his cabinet, disagreements began to show themselves between the Minister of War Ignacio Comonfort, a partisan of a policy of temporizing, and Melchor
Ocampo, whose ideas were radical.

The revolution of Ayutla that raised General Álvarez
to power was an eminently popular and well engineered
movement. The clear-minded liberal spirits who co-
operated with the elderly president represented the
hope of progress for the future of the republic. But
the clergy, as always, continued its obstinate position,
and circumstances compelled Álvarez to resign [in
favor of Comonfort], probably on account of the crime
of having enacted the Law of November 23, 1855,
usually called the Juárez Law [vastly limiting the right
of the Church to maintain separate ecclesiastical
courts]. Actually, the passing of that Law was due to
the great man of Reform, the distinguished patriot
Benito Juárez, one of the eminent men of our country,
a former governor of Oaxaca, who was virulently persecuted by the dictator Santa Anna on account of his
advanced liberal ideas, and who joined the revolution
of Ayutla. In the cabinet of General Álvarez he had
been appointed Minister of Justice, and from this post
he began his offensive against the clergy.

As a result of the promulgation of the Laws of Disentailment [providing that large estates need not be sold intact, but could be subdivided and sold in small portions] active opposition began again. All these circumstances did not, on the other hand, constitute a reason why the clergy should not avail itself of those laws; a Spanish writer, Anselmo de la Portilla, in his book *Gobierno del General Comonfort* narrates the following:

Listen to something that represented the culmination of the scandals of the time. The archbishop suspended the dean of the metropolitan church and two other canons who were highly respected by the chapter and by the city, because they had obtained the award to themselves of the house in which they lived, by availing themselves of the rights granted to them by the Law of Disentailment. Each one of them pleaded in defense that the award had not been made to him, but to a sister; the case became notorious because everyone understood what there really was at the bottom; the liberal journals pointed to the case as evidence of the fact that the Law was not, after all, so very impious. On this same subject, the French historian, Lefebvre, stated that the archbishop of Mexico, while on one hand excommunicating persons to whom the property of the Church was awarded, did not fail privately to advise his own good friends to hasten to acquire such property.

The territory of the nation was again drenched with blood at the instigation of the clergy. A priest, Ortega y García, at Zacapoaztla, under the war cry of "Religion and Privileges" [the word privileges or *fueros* pertained to Church insistence upon maintaining separate ecclesiastical courts] began a revolt, Antonio Haro y Tamariz having later been named as the leader of the movement, and having entered Puebla on January 22, 1856, only to be defeated by Comonfort at Ocotlán. All these happenings did not prevent the holding of the [constituent] congress of 1856. The Minister of Finance, Miguel Lerdo de Tejada, submitted to congress for its approval a bill which stated that as one of the major obstacles in the way of national prosperity and progress was the stagnation or want of free circulation of a great part of the nation's property, the fundamental basis of public wealth, the president had in the exercise of the powers conferred upon him by the Plan of Ayutla decreed the following:

1. All rural and urban real property at present owned or administered by any civil or ecclesiastical corporations in the republic shall be awarded in fee simple ownership to the persons holding them under lease at a value corresponding to the rents at present paid by them, computed at the rate of 6 percent per annum.

2. Similar awards shall be made to those who at present possess rural or urban real property belongings to such corporations on an annuity basis, the payments made by them to be capitalized at 6 percent in order to determine the value of such property.

3. Under the denomination of corporations are included all religious communities of both sexes, brotherhoods and privileged brotherhoods, congregations, confraternities, parishes, city councils, colleges and in general all establishments or foundations the character of which is of perpetual or indefinite duration.

4. Any city real estate directly leased by such corporations to a number of tenants shall be awarded by capitalizing the sum total of the rents paid in favor of the present tenant paying the highest rent, and in the case of there being two or more such tenants, to the oldest. As regards farming property in the same situation, to each leaseholder shall be awarded the portion leased by him.

These first articles of the Lerdo Bill made the archbishop of Mexico state that this congress would not allow him to comply with the law, and he proposed that the matter be referred to the pope for settlement, to which Esequiel Montes replied that the government recognized no one as superior to it to arrange the purely temporal matters of the nation, but that the archbishop could apply to the pope in order to set his conscience at rest. The law was passed by 84 votes to 8.

The draft of the constitution had been read out on July 4, discussion thereof began, and great surprise was caused when the eminent Ignacio Ramírez, whose *nom de plume* was *"El Nigromante"* ("the Magician") objected to the preamble of the constitution in which the name of God was invoked. Those are never to be forgotten words of that eminent master destined to be a subject of meditation by many generations of Mexicans. "The charge of drawing up a constitution is too worthy of respect for me to begin my work with a lie." And so in each one of the provisions of that immortal body of law were incorporated each one of the chief gains of the liberal belief. The constitution was issued on February 5, 1857, and proclaimed on March 17, and orders were given that it be sworn to by the whole of the authorities and public servants of the republic.

Among the bishops who were most exasperated by the proclamation of the constitution and who in open rebellion refused to recognize it, alleging that it contained attacks on the freedom of the Church, the irascible bishop of Michoacán, Clemente de Jesús Munguía, drew on himself unfortunate celebrity by his writings and due to the way in which he registered a protest with the Minister of Justice, refusing to accept the constitution "because it was in opposition to the sovereignty, independence and dignity of our Holy Church," and due to the violence and virulence of the sarcastic attacks in which he gave free rein to his bitterness, calling the new code the apple of discord and many other things. He subsequently retracted those opinions, which he had expressed without the thought and discretion that were necessary.

The clergy then launched a fresh attack on the laws of the republic. Comonfort indulged in dreams of reconciliation, an impossibility from every point of view. His envoy to Rome, Esequiel Montes, was not even received by the Roman pontiff. It was necessary that in the midst of the confusion of political events, a man should arise who would have the courage required to face all the evils afflicting the Mexican state, and the man was Benito Juárez. That notable patriot, as vice-president, lent moral strength to the wavering government of Comonfort. But the clergy was on the lookout for and awaited the turn of political events and its work was crowned by obtaining control of the conscience and will of President Comonfort.

Consequently, under the aegis of Comonfort, Felix Zuloaga [a conservative, proclerical general] seized the capital and disowned the constitution of 1857. Juárez was imprisoned. [Meanwhile, quarreling with Zuloaga] Comonfort was forced to abandon the capital of the republic. Before doing so, he liberated Juárez, who began to plan for reorganization. As the patriot from Oaxaca found himself unable to make resistance to proclerical, conservative Generals Osario and Miramón, he left Guadalajara [whence he had fled from Mexico City] and later on Colima also, and having determined ultimately to reach Vera Cruz he appointed General Santos Degollado as Commander-in-Chief of the Constitutional forces. On April 14, 1858, he boarded a ship at Manzanillo and arrived [after landing at the isthmus of Tehuantepec, proceeding overland to the Caribbean coast and boarding another ship] in Vera Cruz, the traditional liberal stronghold, on May 4 of that same year.

Engaged in his protracted struggle against the conservative forces, Juárez on July 12 issued one of the most important laws of the reform movement: "All the property which the secular and regular clergy have been administering under diverse heads shall become the property of the nation, whatever may be the type of the property or the type of its tenants, or the use to which the property was previously put." In the preamble to the said law is set forth with absolute clearness the cause of the evils afflicting the republic, and the illustrious patriot referred to the criminal interference of the clergy: "If on other occasions some few persons might doubt the fact that the clergy was one of the constant hindrances in the way of the establishment of public peace, today everyone admits that it is in open rebellion against the sovereign."

An eminent Mexican jurist, Jacinto Pallares, has written:

As the clergy owned capital yielding 8 million pesos annually, with dignitaries enjoying emoluments amounting to 130,000 pesos in the case of the Bishop of Mexico, 11,000 in that of the Bishop of Puebla, 11,000 for the Bishop of Michoacán, 90,000 for the Bishop of Jalisco, 35,000 for the Bishop of Durango, etc., with an organization of its own and enjoying a privileged jurisdiction that withdrew it from the national sovereignty, it was not possible for the Mexican government to exact obedience from so powerful a class, when its annual (federal) budget only amounted to 24,000,000 pesos and its president or chief magistrates have never earned more than 36,000 pesos.

The disorder provoked by the religious started up again, but the faith of Juárez is immense, his activity is prodigious, his understanding of the great work he is carrying out clear and precise. At last, he entered the City of Mexico on January 11, 1861, appointed his cabinet, and proclaimed his program.

Juárez then proceeded to dispose of the vast property belonging to the clergy. At the same time the clerical party which, as later graphically expressed in a letter from the Empress Carlota to the Empress Eugénie "would with pleasure abandon its place of honor and its cross, but not its income," attempted to make a supreme effort to overthrow Juárez and to save that property for which it would a hundred times betray the country. Its hatred of Juárez is cleverly described by Émile Ollivier in his book on the French intervention:

The Mexicans rallied round him on account of his personal honesty and the strength of his convictions; all the creoles professing modern ideas followed him. On the other hand, the hatred felt by the reactionary classes and the clergy for that incorruptible and invincible little man, who had risen from such humble origins, was unbounded.

A committee of reactionaries headed by Juan N. Almonte and inspired by the turbulent archbishop of

Mexico, Pelagio Antonio de Labástida, set out for Europe and their machinations did not constitute a source of pride even for the reactionaries themselves. Napoleon the Third was induced to believe that the saner element in Mexico was desirous of allied intervention to restore peace, disturbed by factions described in dismal terms. The same historian [Ollivier] quoted above, who came to Mexico with the French army, after praising Juárez describes the clerical party as follows: "The conduct of the conservatives was very different; they treated their unfortunate land like a country conquered by blood and fire." On the arrival of the invading troops and after they had violated the agreements concluded at La Soledad, the French marched on Mexico, and gradually came to realize the misapprehension into which they had been led, which induced General Lorencez to write down the following words: "We have no one on our side here. The reactionary party, now almost destroyed, is abhorred. The liberals have seized the property of the clergy, which property constitutes the greater part of Mexico."

Notwithstanding the indications received by the French to the effect that they were not welcome, there was one moment (when the metropolitan chapter welcomed the invading army headed by General Elie-Frédéric Forey, the insolent Almonte and the traitor Leonardo Márquez, with a solemn *Te Deum* in the Cathedral) when Forey was able to believe that only an insignificant faction actually opposed the plans of the conservatives, and that the latter did represent the popular will, and for some time he led the Emperor to believe this, all the more as General Forey did not see things through his own eyes but through those of Dubois de Saligny, whom the Emperor had charged him to take for his guide and leader as having a thorough knowledge of the Mexican people and politics.

The clerical commission stayed in Europe and their activities were only evinced by the measures taken by Napoleon and the manner in which he controlled the tactics of the French army, as said commission, the organ and instrument of the clerical party, served as a glass through which the Emperor gazed at the Mexican question, and construed the varied information received by him. Thus it was that although he wished, before taking the Archduke Maximilian's candidacy seriously, that the vote of the inhabitants of Mexico be taken, he succeeded in convincing himself that even if the vote was not absolutely representative yet that it was sufficient to constitute good grounds for awaiting the consolidation of Maximilian's throne. Saligny was a politician allied to the clergy, the one who worked the maneuver for the benefit of the army; and when the provisional government of the regency was established, and the Archduke accepted the throne, Saligny was able to boast that he had raised to power the "retrograde clerical party," as Ollivier called it.

The Emperor Maximilian came and was received with a specious show of solemnity organized by the clerical party, and he was given to understand that he had come to subserve the interests of the conservative party. How great must the surprise of the clericals have been when they found that the Emperor was not disposed to make the protection of the clergy's interests one of his aims, but to pursue a policy of conciliation by ratifying the laws providing for secularization of Church property. This change of course was perhaps not wholly spontaneous, but may have been dictated by Napoleon the Third, as the following quotation from Ollivier would seem to assert:

General F. A. Bazaine [serving then as commander of the French forces in Mexico] proceeded to carry out the new instructions received from the Emperor. He annulled the decree on sequestration and all the other reactionary measures adopted by the regency; and although he postponed the time of giving security to holders of Church property, until Monsignor Labastida should arrive. . . . The latter told him that he had come back for the purpose of *reconstructing the domain seized from the clergy.* Bazaine, nonplussed, answered that his instructions were to the contrary. The prelate replied that he had laid his views before His Majesty, who had seemed to approve them; and that his dignity and conscience forbade him to accept any solution until authorized therefore by the Holy Father. . . . seven bishops joined the archbishop in a protest against what they called the spoliation of the Church, and threatened any one cooperating therein with major excommunication (alluding of course to the Emperor Maximilian himself as well); they reached the point of revealing their true attitude very clearly, by saying without circumlocution that if he recognized the validity of the secularization of the property of the Church, what was the good of the Intervention? That the Emperor had by them been called to repeal the laws of Juárez, not to ratify and execute them.

From the foregoing quotations, and especially from the last which contains statements made by the clergy, no one can have any further doubts as to what was the true meaning of intervention, nor as to who those guilty thereof were, nor as to the responsibility accruing to that baneful and ambitious clergy in the bitterest period of our national history.

When the lawful government of Benito Juárez as provisional president of the republic was again restored [in 1867, following the removal of French troops and the subsequent overthrow of Maximilian's Empire], he addressed to the nation a vigorous and optimistic manifesto:

Mexicans, I congratulate you on the reestablishment of peace and on the rich fruits of the victories achieved by our valiant hosts. . . . Thanks to you who learned to understand and carry through the gigantic enterprise of democracy in Mexico, an armed oligarchy no longer exists in the land of Hidalgo and Morelos, nor that other more terrible oligarchy of the clergy which seemed to be unconquerable due to the influence of time, interests, and prestige. . . . Neither freedom, nor constitutional order, nor progress, nor peace, nor the independence of the nation would have been possible without [the curbing of the Church's temporal powers achieved by] The Reform.

On December 8, 1867, the Fourth Congress declared that Juárez had been elected to the presidency of the republic and Sebastián Lerdo de Tejada to the presiding post of the Supreme Court of Justice.

After being again elected to the presidency, Benito Juárez died on July 18, 1872. His had been a life dedicated to the service of his country. He had proved the saviour of the republican principles embodied in the constitution of February 5, 1857, and he had been able to fulfill this role only by issuing and putting into effect the laws of The Reform. At his death, the Catholic clergy of Mexico had been almost completely defeated, the clergy that had shown itself the bitter enemy of those precepts, and whose representatives, the conservative party, had suffered two tremendous setbacks in the struggle: the first, an economic one, consisting in the nationalization of a great part of its property, real estate and capital loaned on mortgages, with which it had hoped to carry on indefinitely its Civil War, in the hope that victory would imply the abrogation of the constitution and of the laws above mentioned; the second, a political and social one, since the government of the republic had by act of law taken control of all acts pertaining to the civil status of the people, making these acts legally valid without reference to any religious creeds, and definitely establishing complete freedom of worship.

The country appointed as president don Sebastián Lerdo de Tejada, who had ably assisted don Benito Juárez in the bitter struggle against the conservative party, and who in order that the laws of The Reform should not be easily abrogated and to confirm their enforcement, raised them to the rank of constitutional precepts on September 25, 1874, in accordance with the following amendment:

The constitution shall be amended as follows:

Art. 1. The state and the Church shall be independent one from the other. Congress shall not issue laws either establishing or prohibiting any religion whatsoever.

Art. 2. Matrimony is a civil compact. This and any other act pertaining to the civil status of the people shall be vested exclusively in the civil authorities, in the terms by law provided, and shall have the force and validity which these laws bestow on them.

Art. 3. No religious institutions shall acquire real estate nor possess capital to be loaned on mortgages. . . .

Art. 4. A simple promise to speak the truth and to carry out the obligations assumed shall replace the religious oath with its effects and penalties.

Art. 5. The state shall not permit any contract, covenant or agreement to be carried out having for its object the abridgement, loss or irrevocable sacrifice of the liberty of man, whether by reason of labor, education or religious vows. The law therefore does not recognize the establishment of monastic orders nor shall it countenance their existence, whatever be their denomination, or for whatever purpose they be contemplated.

Somewhat later, on December 14, 1874, the organic law relating to the above amendment and reforms to the constitution was issued. It reiterated that a simple affirmation to speak the truth and to carry out the obligations assumed replaces the religious oath with its effects and penalties. At the same time it became indispensable that all officers and employees of the federal government or the state governments, as well as of the municipalities, should make the affirmation as by law provided in order to continue or to enter upon, as the case might be, the discharge of their respective posts.

With the purpose of disobeying the constitution and the laws of The Reform, and of preventing Catholics who held office under the administration from making the affirmation by law provided, the clergy decreed that all those who should make the affirmation would be excommunicated, declaring by means of pastorals of the bishops and by sermons publicly preached by priests that those persons, that is to say Catholics, should not obey the constitution of the republic and the laws above mentioned. But the clergy was not content with these measures and after inciting the Catholic masses to rebellion they provoked various uprisings led by priests in person, especially in the states of Michoacán and Mexico.

The enemies of the president of the republic, don Sabastián Lerdo de Tejada, were very numerous and among them appeared General Porfirio Díaz who had aspired to the presidential office from the time of Juárez. Uprisings succeeded each other and taking advantage of these circumstances, in January of 1876, General Díaz proclaimed the Plan of Tuxtepec.

Not only the partisans of General Díaz but also the discontented followers of Lerdo contributed to the downfall of the president of the republic, and as Article 8 of the revolutionary Plan of Tuxtepec provided that the ranks of the military men would be recognized, many officers who served at the time of the Empire joined the armies of the rebellion; but what is more yet, the Catholic clergy contributed with its wealth since they were the only sector of the community that possessed it, in the hope of obtaining from the new administration the realization of their aims.

The part directly played by the clergy in the Revolution of Tuxtepec can be gathered authoritatively from the various publications alluded to by the author above named,* among which the following selection figures prominently:

The connivance of the Porfiristas with the clergy can be deduced from the tone of *El Constitucional*, a clerical newspaper which said: "The situation of the country cannot be worse. Uprisings are occurring on every side; armed bands exist in various states of the republic; public opinion is unsettled; all the symptoms of a coming revolution make themselves felt. Up to the present the plan supported by the rebels has not been issued and the chief who had led them has not yet appeared on the scene. But what appears most credible is that these uprisings proceed from conservative sources; that we are threatened by a religious struggle provoked by the government, which

---

* This reference is unclear, as it seems impossible to deduce, from either the original Spanish text or the English translation, what author is being cited. [Editor's note]

will be responsible for all the evils that this struggle will entail to the country."

The connivance of the Porfiristas with the clergy has now been made perfectly clear. The Catholic journalist don José Joaquín Terrazas declared in 1885 in his paper *El Reino Guadalupano* that General Porfirio Díaz had agreed with the clergy in 1876 to enter into a concordat with the pope and to abrogate the laws of The Reform provided the clergy should lend him all assistance needed to bring about the downfall of Lerdo de Tejada's government. If this concordat was not entered into it was due to the energetic opposition of liberal politicians whose arguments made an impression on the mind of General Díaz who, when the Plan of Tuxtepec triumphed, declared himself president of the republic.

FÉLIX NAVARRETE

The Conflict in Mexico Between the Civil Power and the Clergy, 1854-1876: Defense of the Clergy

Within a year after the appearance of the 135-page book by Portes Gil, the conservative historian and lawyer Félix Navarrete published a rebuttal of some 240 pages. Navarrete charged that the attack of Portes Gil against the Mexican Church was written in compliance with the wishes of President Lázaro Cárdenas [1934-1940], who was at the time under heavy criticism from the clergy because of his permissive attitude toward the rigorous anticlerical programs being carried out by certain state governors. Cárdenas wished to retaliate, Navarrete surmised, by having the past actions of the clergy distorted and discredited. In the introduction to his book Navarrete stated: "I propose to make a calm and impartial evaluation of the [Portes Gil] study and of the reliability of the authorities cited therein. . . . I trust, then, that my writing will not be judged subversive and seditious, for I do not propose to go beyond the strict limits of sound historical method."

Some of the principal points of contention between Portes Gil and Navarrete involve the right of the state to suppress ecclesiastical courts; the amount of Church

From Félix Navarrete, *La lucha entre el poder civil y el clero a la luz de la historia* (El Paso, Texas, 1935), excerpts from pp. 109-178. By permission of the Revista Católica Press, El Paso, Texas.

wealth in mid-nineteenth century Mexico and the use to which Church property was put after confiscation by the state; the role of the clergy in encouraging French intervention; the legitimacy of the process whereby Maximilian was declared emperor in 1863; and the part played by clergymen in the 1876 revolution led by Porfirio Díaz against President Sebastián Lerdo de Tejada.

LET us take a look at the famous Juárez Law. The section of the law which most directly concerns us stated:

Special courts are eliminated. . . . Ecclesiastical courts will no longer try cases that pertain to civil affairs. They may continue to try cases involving common crimes committed by individuals under their jurisdiction [i.e., clergymen] until a definitive law is issued to regulate the matter.

Well now, the first thing you notice is that the quoted articles contain an attack on ecclesiastical immunities. In effect, it can be historically demonstrated that the privilege of ecclesiastical jurisdiction was already recognized by Constantine the Great, which means that the privilege antedated his reign.

The reverend bishops of the republic naturally protested against the Juárez Law. So that the lawyer Portes Gil cannot get away with his statements about the "rebellious and seditious bishops who were dedicated only to obstructing the work of the government," I have felt it necessary to point out how the Juárez Law was an attack against the very ancient and universally recognized rights of the Church. Thus, the protests of the reverend bishops were purely defensive acts against an unjust and unwarranted attack. Next, I want to state the reasons on which the bishops based their protests. It will then be evident that they were not protesting simply in the desire to hinder the government.

Typical of the stand taken by the Mexican hierarchy was the statement by the reverend archbishop of the country. He averred that the privilege of ecclesiastical courts had applied to all the churches of the republic since their founding. He stated also that the general law of the Church definitely prohibited ecclesiastics, under pain of very severe penalties, from renouncing the legal status that subjected them to the jurisdiction of ecclesiastical courts. He ended with an appeal in his own name and in that of all the reverend bishops:

Since we are certain of your religious faith and of your love and respect for the Holy See and its venerable head the Sovereign Pontiff, we hope that you will pass this matter on to our Most Holy Father, on whose declaration we will depend, since it is not possible for us to go against the general laws of the Church, or to comply in the slightest with any disposition that might contradict them.

One of the most obvious features of the book by the lawyer Portes Gil is unquestionably the tremendous disorder in which it is written: it mixes up and jumbles its points, creating a vortex, a hodgepodge out of which the reader can acquire nothing except a great deal of confusion.

In commenting upon the 1856 Law of Miguel Lerdo de Tejada, the Portes Gil book accepts the proposition that "one of the major obstacles in the way of national prosperity and progress was the stagnation or want of free circulation of a great part of the nation's real estate, the fundamental basis of public wealth."

I do not understand how the lack of movement or free circulation of real property can be at any time one of the major obstacles to the prosperity and progress of a nation. Would this mean that a nation in which the rural farms and urban properties change owners as often as the owners change shirts will be the richest, the most powerful, and the most prosperous one in the universe? I understand the fact that should the owners of rural and urban property allow their estates to remain unproductive they would thereby impair the prosperity of the nation. These unused lands would lead to the unemployment of many men who could be productively utilizing these resources. Unproductive land would also lead to a reduction of agricultural harvests, diminish the value of national exports, and curtail government revenue. If, however, the farms are producing what normally they could, even if the owners do not work them personally but rather have them rented out, I cannot understand why the mere fact that they are retained in the same family or in the same association, even if this should be forever, would impede the progress and prosperity of the nation.

In protesting against the Law of Lerdo de Tejada, the learned bishop of Michoacán, Clemente de Jesús Munguía, began by establishing this indisputable principle: "The property which the Church possesses belongs to it independently of the will of governments; the right to acquire, maintain and administer this property does not proceed from temporal concessions, but rather from the inalienable rights of the institution itself, the Catholic Church." Bishop Munguía added:

The free use of this property, without any exceptions other than those which might arise from the demands of justice, is a right which has always been recognized by organized societies. It is a right which is stressed in the legislation of civilized peoples. It is, therefore, a principle which is derived from the natural law and which is superior to all human law. At the present time, although the Church is deprived of its property, the Mexican law recognizes the right to property ownership, and is even trying to increase the number of proprietors. Why is it, then, when everyone's right to property ownership is recognized as one of his most valuable guarantees, that the Church remains not only without this guarantee, but also dispossessed of its property?

After a mishmash of historical facts, which are not only scrambled but which go by as fast as the frames of a motion picture, the lawyer Portes Gil arrives at the law proclaimed by Juárez on July 12, 1859 [nationalizing Church property without compensation], and praises it as ". . . one of the most important laws of the Reform movement." By way of commenting on the law, Portes Gil copied a paragraph from the lawyer Pallares. I want to say something about the Pallares statement.

The first impression that I received from his passage was such that I exclaimed: "Good gracious, this lawyer with such a talent for juggling figures belongs in the circus!" Really, his display makes the most notorious financial manipulations look like child's play.

After having studied the documents that I have published elsewhere which deal with clerical income since independence, and after having read those records related to the Church's financial contributions during the War with the United States, and taking into account also the Lerdo Law that forced the Church to sell its urban and rural properties, no one could possibly believe that in 1859 the archbishop of Mexico still had an annual income of 130,000 pesos. The only possible conclusion is that lawyer Pallares had no knowledge whatsoever of the pertinent documents. Had he been acquainted with them, surely he would not have printed those fantastic figures. Furthermore, the lawyer Portes Gil could not have been acquainted with them either. Had he been so, he would never have quoted lawyer Pallares.

Well, let lawyer Pallares play the role of the lawyer as much as he wishes. What we have shown proves that as a historian he is not worth two cents. Lawyer Portes Gil, in so far as he indiscriminately includes in his book any argument against the Church which he happens to come upon, without bothering to check its accuracy or to investigate the qualifications of its author, disqualifies himself also as a historian. One might prepare a legal brief with such methods, but the writing of history requires some element of critical ability.

The law published by Juárez on July 12, 1859, in Vera Cruz stated that all of the property which the secular and regular clergy had been administering under diverse heads should become the property of the nation.

I shall quote from what the commission summoned in 1863 to pass judgement upon the form of government that would be most suitable to Mexico had to say about this law of Juárez:

If we reflect upon it, we can see that the alleged progress and reform of recent years have resulted in the destruction of Church wealth and clerical capital. If these great sums of money had been invested in the construction of railroads, in payment of the foreign debt, in the establishment of a bank, or in any of the other things from which the nation might have derived great benefit, perhaps the seizure of so much wealth would have been viewed by the people with less repugnance. But it was not the country that was to gain; nor did society in general receive a single benefit from such disorders; it was only private individuals, those who held public office or who were the hangers-on and sycophants of men in office, who divided up the spoils.

In continuing his study, Portes Gil makes the statement: "At that time the clerical party . . . attempted to make a supreme effort to overthrow Juárez and to save that property for which it would a hundred times betray the country."

Lawyer Portes Gil should realize that no matter how reliable his word might be, and I assume it to be highly reliable, the writing of history can never rest exclusively upon the dogmatic assertions of one individual. Rather, at least a few confirmatory facts must be presented. In the case at hand, as in many others, this requirement which is indispensable to the writing of history is quite forgotten. After telling us quite seriously that the clerical party would betray the country a hundred times, he fails to cite even one single case of such a betrayal. It is hopeless! This time, as I have already done so often, I shall have to remedy the forgetfulness of Portes Gil by referring to some facts and documents.

That the clergy never committed such an ugly crime as the betrayal of their country is proved by the formal and solemn protests which the reverend bishops repeatedly made against this charge. On numerous occasions when the charge was brought against them, they immediately responded by rejecting it outright. Those who ought to have responded—if they had been able—to the denial of the prelates by means of factual refutations, always remained silent. If Comonfort and Juárez could not refute the denials of the bishops, neither can lawyer Portes Gil. We may very well conclude that all of the talk about the treason and betrayal of the country has no applicability to our clergy.

The lawyer Portes Gil goes to considerable length to describe the French intervention in Mexico, basing his account on the testimony of Émile Ollivier. By describing Ollivier as a man who came to Mexico with the French army, Portes Gil seems to imply that the French writer's views upon the intervention must be accepted as absolute truth.

In 1863 José María Gutiérrez Estrada published in Mexico a pamphlet entitled *Méjico y el archiduque Fernando Maximilian*, which throws a rather different light upon the French intervention. According to the preface, the work was written in Paris in November of 1861. Well now, in this pamphlet the author, who had good reason to know, says:

Various foreign ministries of Europe as well as the State Department in Washington received petitions for intervention during the last two years, sent by our citizens of Mexico and, what is more, sometimes signed even by government officials. Those who invited European intervention realized that they were not jeopardizing our sovereignty. Rather, European intervention would defend and strengthen our nation and raise it from the misery into which it had fallen. On the other hand, United States intervention would undoubtedly have ruined our country all the more, bringing us face to face with the inevitable loss of our national sovereignty and independence.

The Assembly of Notables that came together in 1863 in Mexico City to decide upon what form of government was suitable for the country declared: "The nation adopts as its form of government the hereditary, constitutional monarchy, with a Catholic prince as its monarch." This declaration, and the subsequent selection of Ferdinand Maximilian of Hapsburg as the Mexican ruler was perfectly legal. Article 39 of the 1857 constitution, then in force, concluded with the statement: "The people have at all times the inalienable right to alter or modify the form of their government."

Now then, no one will understand the term "the people" to refer to the throngs of illiterates. "The people," says Father Cathrein in his *Filosofía moral*, "considered as a political entity, does not consist of every individual regardless of age and sex, but only of all the citizens in so far as they head and represent their families." Furthermore, His Eminence Bishop Munguía in his elementary course on natural law says:

What is required, then, for one legitimately to participate in the electoral process? First, he must have an understanding of the functions that pertain properly to rulers; second, he must be fully informed about the relative merits and attributes of those seeking political office; third, he must be morally disposed to favor those who are most worthy and virtuous. A background of isolated rural living, the lack of common sense and of public interest, ignorance in certain matters and immorality are impediments to the performing of electoral acts. Those who are encumbered by such incapacities are disqualified from suffrage rights. For the voter, then, understanding and moral virtue are essential, since these are universal and immutable precepts.

If we apply this doctrine to our present electoral battles—but we had better not try that! If we apply this doctrine to the Assembly of Notables and to the act that concerns us, we will have to declare that the electors were true electors; that their acts were perfectly legitimate, and that accordingly the Archduke Maximilian became the legitimate Emperor of Mexico. But, the electors were looking for a Catholic prince, and although Maximilian had all the appearances of such, in reality, neither he nor his political godfather Napo-

leon the Third, the French Emperor, was a Catholic
prince. The electors were therefore greatly disillusioned.
But if they did not discover their error until too late
to rectify it, you cannot criticize them, at least not so
far as their intentions were concerned.

As it turned out, the Emperor Maximilian wanted
the Holy See to sanction nothing less than the illegal
assaults of Comonfort and Juárez. Because the papal
nuncio in Mexico very justly refused to cooperate with
Maximilian in this matter, the Emperor retaliated by
proclaiming a law the first article of which stated: "The
laws and decrease issued before and after independence
concerning the right of the civil authority to control
the admission of bulls, apostolic briefs, rescripts and
dispatches from the curia in Rome are in force in the
Empire."

With the final defeat of Maximilian's forces in 1867,
the liberals under Juárez returned to power. Following
the death of Juárez in 1872, the Sebastián Lerdo de
Tejada administration introduced amendments aimed
at elevating to the status of articles of the constitution
the anticlerical decrees previously issued by Juárez.
His Eminence José María de Jesús Díez de Sollano, the
first bishop of León, published in 1873 a short work
entitled: *Exposición del obispo de León contra el
proyecto de elevar a constitucionales las leyes de Reforma.* Has lawyer Portes Gil ever heard of it? If he
has not it is most regrettable, and it can only be recommended that he read and study it. He may rest assured that in it he will find good, legitimate, philosophical, theological and canonical science. Díez de Sollano
was a wise man in the true sense of the word. In the
cited work, lawyer Portes Gil will find the arguments
employed by the venerable Mexican episcopacy to oppose the elevation of the laws of The Reform to the
status of constitutional provisions. Further, he can
convince himself that if the Mexican clergy was an irreconcilable opponent to incorporating the laws of The
Reform into the constitution, its opposition arose not
from blind and irrational hatred and sectarianism, but

rather from dispassionate thought and calm, compelling reason.

While lawyer Portes Gil as usual does not offer a single proof for his assertions, I will need to support mine, by reproducing just a few short portions of the book by Bishop Díez de Sollano. From the section which the bishop devotes to studying the proposal of religious toleration [which was ultimately provided for by Article 1 of the 1874 constitutional amendments], I cite the following:

The question of toleration has been considered three times in constituent congresses: in 1841, 1847, and 1857. On all these occasions the proposals for toleration were rejected because of the explicit and universal national manifestations against them. Perhaps there has never been a more splendid display of the national will than upon these occasions, especially during the 1847-1848 period. The short works that were published in opposition to religious toleration were many and outstanding. They were written by the nation's leading figures, many of whom were not only laymen but eminently liberal. Scarcely a town failed to send a delegation to the constituent congress to argue against toleration. The petitions delivered by these village delegations bore the signatures of the most respectable residents, including even those of ladies who, ignoring their sex, because they were unable to resist the impulse of their Catholic hearts, made their voices resound in the legislative chamber, even though legally they were denied political rights. These demonstrations made it necessary to cast aside the bill so very much desired by Masonic organizations. It is worth noting that despite the circumstances which seemed so favorable in 1857, an absolute majority in the constituent assembly rejected Article 15. In short, the constituent assembly of 1857 explicitly declared that the national will openly rejected religious toleration; in other words, it asserted that the national will was, as it is today, absolutely Catholic.

The fact is that in order to justify religious toleration in Catholic Mexico it was necessary to assume that the country was divided into different religious sects. Actually, non-Catholic sects did not exist. Even today they can scarcely be found. Because of this false assumption made by the civil power, Catholicism was naturally gravely offended. It was offended by the endeavor to equalize it. What did equalizing it entail? Subordinating it to the false religions which the civil power tried to foster.

The disregard of the popular will by the rulers resulted in civil war. The Mexican people, by peaceful and legal means, first made known their clear and unequivocal opposition to the laws of The Reform. They were ignored. Consequently, they then attempted by force of arms to acquire what they had failed to gain by legal measures.

At a later point in his book lawyer Portes Gil states that the clergy played a direct part in the 1876 Revolution of Tuxtepec, led by Porfirio Díaz against Sebastián Lerdo de Tejada, president of Mexico at the time. Upon my word! This really is a riot! The Plan of Tuxtepec recognized as the supreme law of the nation all of the legislation attacking the Church and the clergy; all of the legislation which the reverend bishops and the Supreme Pontiff Pius IX himself had condemned with their full energy. We are asked to believe that the clergy directly helped to elevate General Díaz, who had committed himself solemnly and publicly to continue the work of the persecution, to the presidency!

What is the documentary proof for this? Lawyer Portes Gil produces only a little quotation from *El Constitucional*, a paper published by those who were in rebellion against Lerdo de Tejada. This paper says of the Díaz uprising:

Up to the present the plan supported by the rebels has not been issued and the chief who has led them has not yet appeared on the scene; but *what appears most credible is that these uprisings proceed from conservative sources; that we are threatened by a religious struggle provoked by the government,* which will be responsible for all the evils that this struggle will entail to the country.

I have copied all of this from the same newspaper copied by Portes Gil; I have underlined [italicized] the words which can give rise to the presumption he entertains. I asked my readers: from the paragraph quoted above and from the words which I have underlined, is the presumption of connivance between the clergy and the Revolution of Tuxtepec warranted? I repeat, *El Constitucional* was the organ of the rebels. If the clergy was conniving with them, it was of elementary prudence to cover up for the clergy, and the greatest of follies to say that the revolution had a conservative basis and the character of a religious war. Relying on the laws of good sense and logic, I say that the characterization of the revolution as a conservative and religious movement which was printed in the very organ of the revolution itself proves that there was never any connivance between the Tuxtepec uprising and the clergy. The assertions of *El Constitucional* were made only to incense the government against the clergy.

FRANCIS MERRIMAN STANGER

Church and State in Peru During the First Century of Independence

The relationship between Church and state in Peru has been rather unusual. Members of the clergy have at various times provided leadership for anticlerical movements, while a majority of the proclerical Conservative Party in congress voted in favor of the constitutional provision that abolished the ecclesiastical fuero in 1857. Moreover, the vast wealth of the Catholic Church in Peru, accumulated from earliest colonial times and carefully preserved and augmented to the present day, has not yet produced a civilian reaction of the type that in other republics had led to the confiscation of ecclesiastical property. These and other features of the Peruvian situation are succinctly described by Francis Merriman Stanger, who received the degree of Doctor en Historia from the University of San Marcos in Lima, Peru, and was in 1927, at the time he published his article, a member of the University of California faculty.

Stanger commented upon the mounting evidences of anticlerical and even antireligious sentiments in Peru, and predicted a resulting diminution of Church influence. His prediction has not been entirely borne out. Conservative elements, in which the Church, the army, and the landowners figure prominently, have managed to repress those movements which have been hos-

From Francis M. Stanger, "Church and State in Peru," *Hispanic American Historical Review*, II, No. 4 (November, 1927), excerpts from pp. 418-437. By permission of the Duke University Press and of the author.

tile to the status quo. The situation is, however, potentially explosive, especially as the influence of Marxism makes headway among intellectual and labor sectors, thus adding to earlier currents of anticlericalism and religious indifference a new menace with which the Church must contend.

THE Peruvian war of independence was the convergence of two revolutionary movements initiated in the southern and northern extremities of the continent and led respectively by José de San Martín and Simón Bolívar. Politically their main purpose was the same—separation of the entire continent from the domination of Spain—but religiously the ideals they represented were quite distinct. In Argentina the patriot leaders were good Catholics and the Church worked in sympathy with the revolution. The patriot general Mariano Belgrano, following ancient Catholic custom, carried out an elaborate ceremony in which his army was blessed and the image of the Virgin of Mercy was made its general in chief. When San Martín organized his Army of the Andes, he imitated Belgrano's ceremony to the letter and made the Virgin of Carmen patron of his army.

In the north all was different, for there the Church was frankly opposed to the revolution and the revolutionary commanders were at the same time leading freethinkers. Bolívar and Antonio José de Sucre, the two great leaders who went from this region to Peru, were representatives of this type of vigorous and energetic freethinking insurrection. Men of their group came to look upon the clergy in general as a royalist force to be reckoned with. Bolívar always showed respect for religion but he held that it was not a subject for legislation, and he desired to found a state in which no religion should be officially recognized.

San Martín's was the first liberating expedition to reach Peru. According to custom, most of the higher clerical positions were held at that time by Spanish prelates while the lower clergy were native creoles of either pure Spanish or mestizo blood. But the attitude of the clergy as a whole toward independence seems to have followed no obvious rule, as would undoubtedly have been the case had independence first come sponsored by anticlerics like Bolívar and Sucre. Archbishop Bartolomé María de Las Heras, though a Spaniard and a venerable representative of medievalism in religion, remained in Lima when the viceroy fled, entered into friendly relations with San Martín and signed with leading citizens the declaration of independence.

Pedro José Chávez de la Rosa, who was bishop of Arequipa from 1789 to 1805, was very liberal and exerted a notable influence over the younger generation of the clergy, teaching a political liberalism that easily developed into separatism when the occasion called it forth. His two most famous disciples were Francisco Javier Luna Pizarro and Francisco de Paula González Vigil, both of whom will receive further attention in these pages.

On the other hand, some of the bishops worked most energetically to maintain the old regime and were forced to abandon their bishoprics, or chose to do so, before the on-coming patriot armies. They were followed by other royalist clergymen. Though there is difference of opinion and no exact data, it is probable that most of the lower clergy, both regular and secular, favored independence. There are instances of priests who took up arms in the patriot cause as did Hidalgo of Mexico, and some of the leading personalities in organizing the new republic were clergymen.

The most notable of these was Luna Pizarro. He was a native of Arequipa, well educated in theology and law, and held high positions in educational institutions and in the cathedral in Lima. He became the most prominent of a group of priests who were penetrated with the ideas of the French Revolution, and leader of the Nationalist Liberal Party. He worked against San Martín's monarchical plans and even favored freedom of worship. He was the first president of a Peruvian congress and for a number of years a dominant figure in the government. In 1845 he was made arch-bishop of Lima and held this position the remaining nine years of his life.

When, as a result of the famous interview between Bolívar and San Martín in Guayaquil [July, 1822], the latter decided to withdraw from Peru, he convoked the first Peruvian congress and surrendered the command of affairs into its hands. Bolívar, who soon after was made dictator, evidently hoped to unite Peru and Bolivia with Ecuador and Colombia under his personal rule in order to weld them into one nation, and was paving the way for that unity by inducing them to adopt similar constitutions. Bolívar's ideas regarding religion and the state are made plain by the following extract from his address to the Bolivian assembly, accompanying the presentation of his proposed constitution:

Legislators: I will make mention of one article which my conscience has caused me to omit. In a political constitution no religious proposition should be proscribed, because, according to the best doctrines on fundamental laws, constitutions are to guarantee political and civil rights, and as religion does not pertain to either of these rights, its nature is indefinable in the social order and it belongs to the moral and intellectual. . . . Applying these conditions, can a state govern the consciences of its subjects? Can it oblige the keeping of religious laws and give rewards or punishments when the tribunals are in heaven and when God is the judge? Only the inquisition would be capable of replacing such courts in this world. Shall the inquisition return with its incendiary torches?

In Peru, Bolívar's plan was nearly successful, for there the religious article simply made Catholicism the religion of the state with no restriction on other religions. This was the most liberal clause to appear in any Peruvian constitution prior to 1915.

Bolívar's government also undertook to establish administrative regulations and reforms with respect to the Church. Certain schools and religious orders accused of royalist sympathies were broken up or their funds confiscated; all the regular clergy were ordered to submit to the administration of the bishop of their diocese; no monastery could be maintained without at least eight monks in actual residence; minors could not enter a monastic order; the number of religious holidays was reduced, etc.

Bolívar had no more than left the country [1826] in charge of his appointees and gone to attend to affairs elsewhere than a reaction set in against him and his constitution. Although this reaction brought with it a certain religious conservatism, the causes were political as well as religious. The idea of a dictatorship in time of peace, his having been named president for life, and his evident ambition to unite different countries under his personal rule wounded liberal and nationalistic sentiments. As a result, the Nationalist Liberal Party on one hand and the reactionary element on the other united against what was called the tyranny of Bolívar.

This anti-Bolivarist movement developed into a complete and pacific revolution. A new constituent assembly was called and proceeded to frame a constitution under the presidency of Luna Pizarro. In this the article appears which declares: "The religion of the state is the Apostolic Roman Catholic; the nation protects it by all the means in keeping with the spirit of the gospel, and will not permit the exercise of any other." Some of the reforms of the previous government were confirmed while others were ignored as illegal.

The period of Ramón Castilla's domination [1845-1862], in which order was maintained but large freedom of expression permitted, saw the first serious attempt at republican government. It was in this epoch that a new party division appeared, the two groups being known as liberals and conservatives. The question of federalism versus centralization never seriously affected Peru, as it did some other Hispanic-American countries. The dispute here was between centralized conservatism and popular idealistic liberalism.

The leaders of both parties recognized the national

weaknesses but, with equal sincerity and fervor, proposed different remedies. The conservatives would put an end to anarchy by means of a strong centralized government. They would offset the ignorance of the masses with the brilliance and wisdom of an educated class, especially prepared to govern. Moral evils they would correct by giving prestige and vitality to the Church. The liberals, on the other hand, proposed to remedy the general political and social confusion by democratic organization. Ignorance they would cure, not offset, by popular education, while as to morality, they considered the Church incapable of moralizing because of having set, as they said, the first example of immorality. It was the old question of classes versus the democratic ideal, with the clerical dispute included.

The leaders of both parties were of the intellectual, well-to-do class, socially far removed from the ignorant masses. The conservatives saw the hope of the country in their own class while the liberals had a vision of true popular sovereignty. They recognized the wide difference between their ideal and the actual reality but they hoped to make progress by popular education and political experimentation. To bring this about they demanded certain immediate reforms, most important of which were a large measure of popular and local sovereignty, religious tolerance, non-clerical public schools, the abolition of the ecclesiastical *fuero*, and relief of the Indians from the abusive system of tithing.

It will be noted that a great part of the reform measures demanded were directed against the clergy. It is probably this fact that accounts for the absence of the clergy in the liberal party. The liberalism of Luna Pizarro, the cleric, had been inherited by laymen and the outstanding leader of the conservatives was now a priest. It is this division of opinion that seems to have been the more natural alignment for, with varying names and standards, it has persisted to the present day.

[An exception to the general pattern of clerical opposition to the liberal party was a] figure already mentioned. Vigil, one of the younger liberal friars at the time of the War of Independence, was now in elderly life but unchanged in his ideas. He had been an outstanding figure in his group but was now, as among the clergy, living in practical ostracism. In personality he was quiet but fearless. He was repeatedly a member of congress and was later the national librarian. His claim to renown is his voluminous work entitled *Defense of the Authority of Governments and Bishops against the Pretensions of the Court of Rome,* which was condemned and prohibited by that court. His fame rests not so much upon the work itself, which was but little read, but on his refusing to be silenced by the condemnation. He calmly wrote and published a reply, boldly refuting, one by one, the propositions of the papal condemnation. His greatest contribution to liberalism was undoubtedly his furnishing an example of a friar and a Peruvian who refused to be intimidated by ecclesiastical censure.

It was the congress of 1856, controlled by the liberals, that first passed a resolution to abolish the *fuero* constitutionally. It was adopted after a long and heated debate. But the whole constitutional revision, containing many of the political doctrines of the liberals, was submitted for approval and legalization by popular oaths of allegiance. The result, instead of strong popular approval as the liberals hoped, was only a prolongation of the debate and ultimate failure. The opposition of the clergy and other conservatives prevented legalization until a political shift had placed the control of congress in the hands of the conservatives and the whole situation was changed. A new revision of the constitution was made and the work of the liberals was undone. But, to the surprise of many, the abolition of the *fuero* was maintained by an emphatic majority, against the determined opposition of Bartolomé Herrera, leader of the conservative party, and president of the congress. The conservatives, not so much committed to the ideals of popular sovereignty, did not submit their constitution to the people but simply declared it in force by act of congress. The *fuero* then ceased to be a factor in Peruvian politics.

The only notable alteration of the economic affairs of the Church by legislation has been the abolition of the Indian tithes, and in this the interests of the Church were carefully guarded. The motive was not primarily to attack the economic power of the Church but to improve the conditions of the Indian by ending a long-standing abuse. Measures were taken to reassure the Church and to avoid its hostility. By act of the congress of 1859 the collection of tithes was prohibited and the government made itself responsible to the Church for the amount the tithes had produced.

Another important matter that has been gradually taken from the hands of the Church, where it was placed by Spanish law, is the control of cemeteries. The idea that the place and circumstances of burial have directly to do with the happiness of the deceased in the next world has furnished one of the clergy's most effective means of control over the people, by the granting or refusal of interment in ground consecrated by the Church.

The establishment of municipal cemeteries in Peru was begun soon after the winning of independence and was probably promoted by the Church because of the expense involved in providing more burial space. But under municipal control, the liberal and anticlerical elements had a voice in the matter and could bring pressure for the adoption of a more liberal attitude toward non-Catholics. Those who could think of a Peruvian as non-Catholic were, in the early days, very rare, if they existed at all, but an increasing body of people demanded the same consideration and respect for non-Catholic foreigners who died in the country as was given to those of their own religion. This was an evident necessity if desirable foreign trade and immigration were to be promoted. From this entering wedge has come a liberalization of public opinion and practice that has placed the cemeteries generally under the control of the municipalities.

More recent reforms in religious affairs were the passing of the civil marriage law (1897) and the constitutional amendment granting religious liberty (1915). The Peruvian civil code recognized no form of marriage other than the rites established by the Council of Trent. Marriage was thereby considered a religious sacrament, a union to be made or dissolved only by the Church. The ecclesiastical monopoly of marriage has been broken by the civil marriage law, but divorce does not exist except as defined by the Catholic Church. Up to 1915 there could legally be no religious tolerance, for the exercise of cults other than the Catholic was forbidden by constitutional law. However, no law had ever defined offenses or established penalties. The amendment of that date suppressed the prohibitory clause, continuing the Church in its official relation to, and under the protection of the state.

Both these reforms were strongly resisted by the Church, and though it could muster only a ridiculously small vote in the congress, obstructionist tactics and diplomatic channels were used and pressure was brought to bear on individuals. The executive was quite obviously under its influence. Clerical authorities were willing, in the end, to sanction a law to permit the legalization of the marriage of non-Catholic foreigners, but the principles of civil marriage and religious liberty were bitterly opposed.

Both reforms were occasioned by events that had aroused a storm of public protest. A North American couple, married in Peru, were denied legalization of their union. Their appeal to the president and his refusal gave wide publicity to the affair and resulted in action by congress. It began with the purpose of providing accommodation for non-Catholic foreigners and ended in the civil marriage law. The other reform was the direct result of a mob attack on a Protestant mission among the Indians, organized and led by the bishop of Puno. In both cases overwhelming majorities in congress favored the reforms and made them effective over the heads of reluctant executives.

Since 1915 no important new adjustments in religious matters have taken place. The separation of Church and state has not been officially proposed in Peru except by the student federation, but clerical influence over public opinion is notably on the wane.

The most cursory glance over the events related in the history of the republic shows that the development has been definitely and consistently toward the reduction of clerical influence. The consistency of the development is in contrast with that of other countries of equal geographical isolation and late-blooming religious liberalism. While Ecuador has seen violent reactions from a strong anticlerical government to the most extreme of ultramontane devotion to Rome, and while Colombia is still obliged by a concordat to permit clerical control of her national school system, Peru has steadily moved away from Roman Catholic domination.

The last half century [keep in mind that the article was published in 1927] has seen the growth of a group among the intellectuals that is not only anticlerical but irreligious, of whom the highest type is Manuel González Prada. These modernists are quite different from the men who protested their loyalty to the Church while they fought its control in politics. The latter were not less religious than their opponents but more independently religious. But to their grandsons irreligion has become a religion and they glory in their devotion to it. The group has spread beyond the bounds of the intellectual class and includes an ever-growing number of those who follow with varying degrees of thought and interest but all of whom are no longer devoted to the Church.

It would be a mistake to conclude that the Church is now a minor factor in Peruvian affairs. Its wealth and extensive ownership of property seem never to have been a matter of popular interest, but they are no less a source of power than in countries where violent agitation and wholesale confiscation have taken place. In politics, presidents and dictators recognize that the support of the Church is quite necessary to a stable government. It is a significant fact that repeatedly executives have been unwilling to even promulgate anticlerical laws passed by the congress. Usually, anticlerical opinion is inarticulate and dormant but becomes overwhelmingly aggressive in response to stimulus. The Church, on the other hand, is an organized force that can apply pressure when and where it chooses, and it usually works through individuals in strategic positions. In the face of the disintegrating effects of modern irreligious tendencies, its organization is its source of greatest strength.

The situation in Peru contains the same seeds that have borne some fruit in other countries of like origin. Different environments have produced slightly different growths, but the ripened product, when it appears, may be expected to bear in each case essential marks of similarity.

CLARENCE H. HARING

The Church-State Conflict
in Nineteenth-Century Brazil

In writing on the most important manifestation of
Church-state conflict in nineteenth-century Brazil, Clarence H. Haring manifests refreshing detachment. Rather
than picturing the event as the result of a clash between thoroughly good and thoroughly evil men, he
sets it in its historical context. Given the extraordinary
powers which the state exercised over the Church in
colonial times, legal conflict was bound to ensue when
the Vatican and certain Brazilian churchmen sought to
enlarge the sphere of papal authority over Church affairs, a movement that was underway throughout the
Catholic world in the second half of the nineteenth
century. Even when men of moderation argued the
matter, the unique circumstances of the historical background, not always appreciated either in Rome or in
the New World, scarcely permitted them to proceed
moderately. Born in 1885, Haring taught courses in
Latin American history and economics at Bryn Mawr,
Clark, and Yale before joining the faculty at Harvard
in 1923. He was appointed professor emeritus at Harvard in 1953. Haring conducted research in Spain and
Latin America and published extensively. He died in
1960, one of the most respected authorities on Latin
American history that the United States has produced.

Reprinted by permission of the publisher from Clarence H.
Haring, *Empire in Brazil. A New World Experiment with
Monarchy*, Cambridge, Mass.: Harvard University Press, copy-
right 1958, by the President and Fellows of Harvard College.
(Excerpts from pp. 113-125.)

ANOTHER traditional buttress of monarchy in Brazil, as in the Old World, was the official Church, always a citadel of conservatism. This support was weakened by a quarrel with the crown over Freemasonry and the imperial control of ecclesiastical administration. The Constitution of 1824 recognized an official religion, Roman Catholic and Apostolic; and the Papacy for its part accepted the *Padroado*, or right of ecclesiatical patronage inherited by the imperial crown from its Portuguese predecessor. As received from the Pope in the sixteenth century, this was primarily the right to nominate to church benefices, and to require royal permission for the publication within the kingdom of any communications from the Roman Curia. But through the medium of regalistic lawyers, especially in the eighteenth century, the prerogatives had been vastly extended. In short, the Church as a corporation had been transformed into a servant of the secular power as a department of state.

The Brazilian clergy by and large were very liberal, and appeared to accommodate themselves easily to this situation. Many of them were active in the Masonic Order. In the republican revolts in Pernambuco in 1817 and 1824, members of the clergy appeared prominently among the leaders. And they enjoyed generally a great prestige, played an important role in the political parties and in parliamentary debates of the first half of the century. The prelates were usually men of a high order, morally and culturally. But as in colonial times most of the rank and file led rather scandalous lives. Clerical celibacy scarcely existed. Indeed, the Minister of Justice, Aureliano de Sousa, in a letter to Fabbrini, the papal delegate, in 1834, declared that the government might abolish at its pleasure such matters of discipline as clerical celibacy, which, he said, "does not exist anyway."

Although the crown never succeeded in negotiating a formal concordat with Rome, the Holy See did not deliberately antagonize the imperial government. In fact, it even gave consent to mixed marriages in Brazil, requested in order to encourage Protestant immigration, a concession never granted to the nations of Spanish America. On the other hand, since the publications of the famous *Syllabus* of Pope Pius IX in 1864, ultramontane influences [advocating the replacing of national with papal authority over Church affairs] had spread among the secular clergy, many of whom, under the direction of several eminent and virtuous bishops, displayed a new spirit of discipline and moral earnestness.

The *Syllabus* claimed for the Church the control of all culture, of science, and of the whole educational system. It rejected liberty of conscience and of worship, and demanded complete independence of the Church from state control. Indeed, ultramontanism, as revived in the nineteenth century, went a step farther and maintained that it was the duty of the state to carry out the wishes and instructions of the Papacy. To that extent the state was subordinate to the Church, a union of altar and throne in which the altar controlled the throne. And this doctrine was accentuated by the proclamation by an Ecumenical Council in 1870 of the Infallibility of the Pope. It was these circumstances that engendered the Kulturkampf in Germany in the 1870's and the emergence of the so-called "Old Catholic" opposition. A similar quarrel was to plague Brazil.

Until 1872 no serious religious conflict disturbed the peace of the country. The apple of discord was the incompatibility of the Papacy and Freemasonry, brought to a head by an encyclical of Pope Pius in 1864, to which the *Syllabus* had been attached, denouncing the Masonic Order. In Brazil it never received the requisite imperial sanction. Masonic lodges flourished in Brazil; they had played an important part in the independence movement. But the old revolutionary spirit in them had long ago disappeared. In no sense had they been anti-religious or anti-Catholic, as in many parts of the Old World.

The first incident occurred in Rio de Janeiro in March 1872. A priest, Father Almeida Martins, deliv-

ered an address at a meeting of the Grand Lodge called
to commemorate the passage of the Law of Free Birth
[granting freedom to those born of slave mothers upon
attaining twenty-one years of age] the year before. His
bishop ordered him to forswear Masonry on pain of
suspension. Almeida failed to comply, and when the
bishop hesitated to carry out his threat, Almeida defied
his superior by celebrating a Mass ordered by a Masonic
lodge. And the conflict was on.

The Masons retorted by bitter attacks in pamphlets
and in the press against the clergy. The challenge was
picked up by Bishop Vital María Gonçalves de Oliveira
of Pernambuco, an ardent and devoted young Capuchin
friar educated in France, recently consecrated, and imbued with ultramontane doctrines. When in June the
Masons of Recife announced a Mass to celebrate the
anniversary of the lodge's founding, Bishop Vital forbade his clergy to officiate at any Mass under Masonic
auspices. Most of the clergy obeyed. But when the
irmandades, religious brotherhoods composed of laymen, were ordered in December to expel their Masonic
members as excommunicated persons, they refused. The
bishop thereupon suspended the religious functions of
the Brotherhood of the Santíssimo Sacramento, and
placed its chapel under an interdict. In a pastoral letter
earlier in the year, he had denounced not only Freemasonry but the *Padroado* as well.

The Brotherhood of the Santíssimo Sacramento appealed to the crown, and in June 1873, after long and
scrupulous consideration by the Council of State presided over by the Emperor, the government ordered
Bishop Vital to remove the interdict within a month.
Meantime the bishop had written to the Pope, who
replied on May 29 recommending the suspension of
the ecclesiastical censures for a year, but if worst came
to worst, excommunication of the Masonic Order, dis-
solution of the rebellious brotherhoods, and organization of new ones. This brief, in defiance of the law,
Bishop Vital published, and he not only refused to
submit to the imperial order but suspended his dean

(who happened also to be a Mason) because he accepted from the president of the province the post of director of one of the public schools. The result was a hostile street demonstration in which the Jesuit college was sacked and the machinery of two Catholic newspapers destroyed. Meantime the bishop was suspending from their religious functions other brotherhoods of Recife until by September 1873 all had been put under interdict except three. The government replied by directing the civil authorities to oblige the clergy to proceed with religious services despite the bishop, but had no success. It therefore on September 27 ordered legal action to be brought against Bishop Vital for violating the Constitution and the Criminal Code.

Meanwhile there were public, and often sanguinary, disorders in the provinces, by Catholic fanatics on one hand, by anti-Jesuit demonstrators on the other, incited by the public press for and against the bishop. In Parliament and in the highest social circles sentiment was divided. Among those supporting the government opinions varied as to the penalties that should be imposed. Some were for sequestering the "temporalities," i.e., revenues ecclesiastical and private; others counseled the expulsion of the bishop from the country as the contumacious official of a foreign power. In December Bishop Vital was ordered brought to Rio for trial by the Supreme Court of Justice, and a fortnight later he was arrested under protest in his palace in Recife and transported on a ship of war to the capital. On February 21, 1874, he was condemned to four years imprisonment at hard labor and costs. The Emperor shortly after commuted the sentence to simple imprisonment.

Bishop Vital had been joined in his crusade by the Bishop of Pará, Antônio de Macedo Costa, a Sulpician of notable but intolerant personality who was already in conflict with the Liberal Party in his own diocese. Three years older than Bishop Vital, and like him educated in France where Freemasonry had always been anticlerical, he never understood that its spirit and objectives in Brazil were the inverse of those in Europe.

The battle began with the publication of a pastoral letter on March 25, 1873, ordering the brotherhoods to dissociate themselves completely from Freemasonry on pain of interdict. The results were similar to those in Pernambuco: appeal of the brotherhoods to the crown, deliberation by the Council of State, and orders in August to remove the interdicts within fifteen days; peremptory defiance by Bishop Macedo, and legal proceedings against him in November. Arriving in Rio de Janeiro in May 1874, on July 1 he received in the Supreme Court the same sentence as that meted out to Bishop Vital.

The conflict between the imperial government and the bishops in Brazil has been followed in some detail because it had important bearings upon concurrent procedures abroad at the Papal Curia. In August 1873 the government decided to appeal directly to the Holy See. Carvalho Moreira, Barão do Penedo, minister resident in London, was entrusted with a special mission to Rome to induce the Papacy to counsel peace and advise the bishops to conform to the Constitution and the laws. The mission seemed even to Penedo to be a hopeless one in view of the uncompromising position taken by Pope Pius and the Church since the publication of the *Syllabus* of 1864, especially as his instructions took the form virtually of an ultimatum. Penedo was informed that the government had ordered the trial of Bishop Vital, and was prepared if necessary to take even more energetic legal measures without awaiting the results of the mission. The government sought no favors, it only wanted justice, and would enter into no compromise. If questioned in these respects, the Ambassador was to state frankly what had been communicated to him.

Barão do Penedo, one of Brazil's most intelligent and accomplished diplomats, pursued a more circumspect course and found in the papal Secretary, Cardinal Antonelli, a friendly and understanding spirit. Pope Pius was apparently persuaded that, on the one hand, in sending Bishop Vital the brief of May 29 he had been misinformed; and on the other, that his recommendation of mildness and restraint in the application of ecclesiastical censures the bishop in his exaggerated zeal had pointedly ignored. It appears that in conversation with Antonelli it was agreed that the Secretary in the Pope's name should write an admonishing letter in this sense to the bishop, to be delivered by the Apostolic Nuncio in Rio. Such a letter drawn up in Latin in December 1873 was read by Antonelli to the Ambassador, who hastened to inform his government of its purport: the Pope was pained by the actions of the bishop, who had misunderstood his letter of May 29; had he consulted with the Holy Father in season, the latter would have been spared this grief; the Pope had recommended moderation and clemency, but the bishop had persisted in the path of severity. The Pope therefore ordered him to restore things as they had been before the peace of the Church was disturbed.

It appeared to be a complete diplomatic victory for the mission. However the Pope had earlier let it be understood that he expected the imperial government on its part to reciprocate by removing all the obstacles to the prompt restoration of peace. And Penedo had assured the Papacy of the conciliatory disposition of his government. News of the arrest of Bishop Vital, therefore, was a shock to both the Ambassador and the Pope. Penedo saw the whole structure of his diplomacy fall to the ground. He had been informed of the intentions of the government in his instructions, but was probably warranted in presuming that they would not be carried into effect. Pope Pius was justifiably indignant, and sent a message to the Emperor urging him to set the bishops at liberty. At the same time orders were dispatched to the Nuncio in Rio to destroy the admonishing letter which already was in the hands of the imprisoned bishops. Its existence, however, had been divulged by the government, which now sought by negotiation in Rome to oblige the bishops to disclose the letter and fulfill its admonitions, under the circumstances a hopeless endeavor.

The Penedo mission and the suppressed papal letter gave opportunity for a vituperative and long-drawn out campaign against the Ambassador and the government. Penedo was accused of having deceived the Pope as to the ultimate intentions of his superiors, or of having reported inaccurately the contents of a letter which he had not himself read. There is no doubt that the Papacy, in spite of the maladroitness of the imperial government in its instructions, had counted on the princely generosity of the Emperor to hold up any peremptory action against the bishops. The imprisoned bishops and their partisans denied that the letter had been written and accused the government of criminal levity in divulging a nonexistent document in order to humiliate them. By implication Penedo was an "unscrupulous inventor of apostolic letters." To many, the actions of the Roman Curia seemed ambiguous. It was not clear whether the Holy See supported the apostolic zeal of the bishops, or thought it preferable to spare the refractory brotherhoods. Echoes of the controversy have come down to our time.

The arrest and imprisonment of the bishops was clearly a blunder, in its inception and its procedure. The prejudices of the Supreme Court were obvious. The Emperor himself was not in the least inclined to indulgence. He approved of the government's course throughout; indeed it is said that he made known his wishes to the judges of the Supreme Court. The bishops had defied the Constitution, flouted the imperial authority and the national dignity. Dom Pedro was by conviction and by tradition a regalist. The vehemence and intolerance of the bishops had made the question a personal matter in which the honor of the crown was also involved. And most of the members of the Council of State shared this regalistic attitude, regarding the insubordination of the bishops as a brazen attempt, inspired by a foreign government, to usurp powers that incontestably belonged to the sovereign authority.

The points of view of the two parties, Church and state, were irreconcilable from the outset, and it would have been better for the peace of the nation and the welfare of the monarchy had the imperial government been content with the administrative penalty of sequestering the temporalities of the bishoprics, as indeed had been suggested in the Council. At least the government had excellent justification for halting the prosecution when it received from Barão do Penedo of the papal letter censuring the bishops and ordering the suspension of the interdicts. The severe punishment decreed against them, on the contrary, not only called forth the vigorous protest of the Apostolic Nuncio and a sharp reproof from Pope Pius addressed personally to the Emperor, but left the bishops confirmed in their obduracy. The interdicts remained, clergy hostile to the government were assigned to diocesan vacancies, and the nation was brought close to the verge of a religious war. In Pernambuco and Pará governors of the diocese appointed by the condemned bishops and recognized as such by the provincial authorities, when they refused to raise the interdicts, were in turn prosecuted and condemned. And as the imperial government refused to accept any others designated by the bishops, as the cathedral chapters ignored orders to appoint vicars general to administer the dioceses, and provincial presidents therefore hesitated to recognize parochial appointments, the consequence was ecclesiastical anarchy.

The only reasonable way out of the impasse was a commutation of the prison sentences, even though it meant the retreat of the government. The Conservative ministry of Rio Branco, which had been in office since 1871, fell in June 1875, and the ministry that followed under the presidency of the Duque de Caxias, also a high-degree Mason, had the courage to face the issue. One of its first steps was to insist with the Emperor that the bishops be pardoned, and on September 17, 1875, the decree of amnesty was issued, against Dom Pedro's personal wishes. The Papacy responded promptly with an order to lift the interdicts and restore the *irmandades* to the *status quo ante*, although this action was accompanied by the customary condemnation of Freemasonry. And Cardinal Antonelli, to the embarrassment of the bishops, publicly transmitted to them a copy of the famous suppressed letter. Owing to the recalcitrance of Bishop Macedo, the penalties imposed on the brotherhoods of Pará were not revoked until 1880. On the other hand, the total exclusion of the Masons from the *irmandades* of Brazil was never carried into effect.

The crusading Bishop Vital retired to Europe, where he died of tuberculosis of the larynx in the following year in Paris. The bishop of Pará was later elevated to the dignity of archbishop primate of Bahia, and as such witnessed the fall of the monarchy and the proclamation of the Republic. But the bitter resentments occasioned by the religious dispute were slow in healing. Whatever the outcome, the monarchy was bound to suffer. The liberals attacked the Emperor because he gave way and pardoned the bishops. The clergy and the conservatives were scandalized by the arrest and humiliation of the churchmen. The republicans, certainly not proclerical, cheered from the sidelines any development that embarrassed the crown. The consequence was an accentuation of antimonarchical opposition that drew support from the discontented on all sides. Insofar as the clergy felt alienated from the crown, one of the traditional props of monarchy had been seriously undermined.

J. LLOYD MECHAM

A Survey of the Church-State Conflict in Latin America During the First Century of Independence

J. Lloyd Mecham has taught in the political science department at the University of Texas since 1925 and has compiled a notable list of publications. He has conducted research in Latin America and Spain. In 1934 he published the classic study of Church and state in Latin America. Whereas Clarence H. Haring pointed out that colonial traditions made legal disputes between Church and state in Brazil inevitable, Mecham, in the concluding section of his book reproduced below, observed that the historical background made political discord between the two powers inevitable. Many Catholic writers in Latin America would not agree with Mecham's conclusion that separation of Church and state is the ideal arrangement. They would also incline to argue that the political issues in which the Church interfered were not purely political, but instead basically moral and therefore within the Church's sphere of competence.

THE ecclesiastical policies of the various Latin-American nations presented marked divergencies. In some countries, like Argentina, Colombia, and Peru, the old Church-state relationship that existed in the colonial

From J. Lloyd Mecham, *Church and State in Latin America* (Chapel Hill, North Carolina, 1934), excerpts from pp. 502-508. By permission of the University of North Carolina Press.

period has been perpetuated, but with certain modifications. In other nations, such as Brazil, Chile, Cuba, Panama, and Uruguay, the connection between Church and state has been dissolved, and a situation rather similar to that which exists in the United States obtains. In still other countries, of which Mexico is the best example, the Church has not only been disestablished, but has been put under strict state surveillance. That a predominantly Roman Catholic populace, which lived for centuries under a common politico-religious regime, should, after independent governments had been organized, apply such diverse remedies for the solution of the religious problem, is both interesting and perplexing.

When embarking upon their independent careers the nations of Latin America adhered for a time to uniformity in religious policy, i.e., Catholicism continued to be the state religion. Indeed, with the sole exception of Argentina (then called the United Provinces of La Plata) religious toleration to the extent of allowing the public exercise of dissident faiths was not among the guarantees of the first national constitutions. Thus, when the youthful nations of Latin America undertook the direction of their own destinies, they were faithful to the religious policy of the Motherland.

Yet, in a short time opposition to the favored cult appeared and it began to be shorn of its old-time privileges. In the decades of the 1820's and 1830's the Catholic Church was subjected to attack in many of the republics, particularly in Argentina, Chile, Mexico, and the Federation of Central America. What was the cause of this traditional change in ecclesiastical policy?

The basis of this early opposition to the Roman Catholic organization—not the Roman Catholic religion—was largely political. The abolition of tithes, suppression of religious orders, confiscation of ecclesiastical property, and like measures were, as a rule, acts of vengeance wreaked upon the clergy by their political opponents. As was explained, the Spanish crown leaned heavily upon the members of the ecclesiastical organization for the governance of the Indies. Prelates and clerics held official positions high and low; they were a component part of the political organization. If it is not charitable to criticize too severely the failure of Latin Americans to govern successfully under representative political institutions, considering their tutelage for centuries under an absolute monarch, it is likewise unfair to expect the clergy to abandon immediately their ancient practice of participating in governmental affairs. It was inconceivable that this habit should be changed forthwith when independence was established. On the contrary, the ecclesiastics plunged into politics with greater zeal than before, for they felt, quite correctly, that their rights would be endangered in representative republics.

But those who engaged in Latin American politics, particularly as it was played in the early days of independence, ought to have been prepared for the consequences of defeat. The opposition, let it be known, was hardly ever "honorable," but was regarded as an enemy of the state and was generally meted the punishment of traitors. Since the clergy who adhered to colonial tradition and chose to take part in political questions were often so unfortunate as to be on the losing side, they frequently suffered the fate of the defeated opposition. Their rights and prerogatives were curtailed in order to nullify their ability to exercise political influence in the future.

These early anticlericals were not reformers in the proper sense of the term. Their opposition was not based on spiritual, social, or economic causes. The "reformers," recruited almost exclusively from the creoles, had no complaint to find with Catholic dogmas and tenets; representatives of a privileged social class, they manifested little interest in the welfare of the lower classes; and if they regarded clerical wealth as an evil, it was because this wealth made the Church powerful politically. The pose of the anticlericals as champions of representative government, the rights of the masses, and purity of the faith was often insincere and untrue.

Usually their sole object was to acquire control of the government and make it impossible to oust them. It is conceded that there were sincere reformers, but such men were exceptional, and unfortunately they were impractical idealists who by unwise and precipitate action caused much more harm than good.

With the passing of the mid-nineteenth century, the position of the Catholic Church in Latin America became increasingly unstable. In Mexico, Colombia, Venezuela, Chile, Ecuador, and Central America, severe anticlerical laws were put into force, and in several of the republics Church and state were separated. The first republic to proclaim separation was Colombia in 1853. This status proved to be temporary, however. The first republic permanently to disestablish the Church was Mexico, but that state was unwilling to release the Church and continued to exercise an oppressive supervision over it. Soon after Mexico, some of the Central American republics disestablished the Church, but intolerantly burdened it with strict state control. In 1890, in Brazil, the alliance of Church and state inherited by the Empire from Portugal was dissolved. In the twentieth century the trend toward separation has continued. Cuba and Panama, states which came into existence under the tutelage of the United States at the beginning of the century, provided in their constitutions for complete separation. In Ecuador only a quarter of a century after the most extreme clerical reaction in all the history of Latin America [directed by Gabriel García Moreno], ecclesiastical policy was carried to the other extreme and the official ties between the spiritual and temporal orders were severed. In 1917 Uruguay dissolved the old connection, formed in 1830. The most recent and one of the most serious losses sustained by the Pope was the separation of Church and state in Chile [in 1925].

The revolutionary step of disestablishing the Church was accomplished peacefully in Brazil, Uruguay, and Chile. In these three important countries the Church was allowed to retain its property unconditionally, and to go its own way without governmental interference [although the Chilean Church in particular has complained about government interference in the private, Catholic schools]. Apparently the policy of releasing the Church properties and observing a minimum of surveillance contributed to the peaceful and seemingly successful transition. In Mexico, however, a contrary policy was adopted with most unfortunate consequences. Since the position occupied by the Catholic Church in that country was not appreciably different than in other Latin-American countries, it does not necessarily follow that the bestowal of complete independence upon the Mexican Church would have been followed by the same happy results. The activities of the clergy during the Maximilian period certainly proved that the time had not arrived to establish an independent Church. Since that time, however, the Mexican clergy have evidently learned their lessons, and at the present date it would probably be safe to allow the Catholic Church the same rights it enjoys in Brazil and Chile.

Citizens of the United States unacquainted with the facts have been too prone to regard Mexico as the only rebellious member of the Catholic flock in Latin America. That this is not true has been conclusively demonstrated. In Venezuela, Colombia, Ecuador, and Chile, the Church was attacked, sometimes with considerable animosity. In several of the lesser countries too, like Guatemala, El Salvador, and Honduras, the same vicissitudes were suffered. Although the attacks in Mexico were more bitter and the results more disastrous, to say that the Mexican remedies were more severe because the abuses were more glaring would not be absolutely true. In other countries the Church was quite as wealthy, relatively speaking, and as much of a political factor.

A significant feature of the religious conflicts has been the uncompromising attitude of the opposing factions. The difficulty intrinsically is not insuperable, as is evidenced by its satisfactory settlement in several of the countries through the application of a policy of mutual respect and fair play. But in many of the nations of Central and South America the intolerance of clericals and anticlericals alike makes a solution well nigh impossible. Neither side is willing to concede any errors in its own program or virtues in that of the opposition. Consequently, as history reveals, there has been a constant ebb and flow of clerical and anticlerical opposition.

It would not be correct to contend that the anticlerical assault of the last three quarters of a century continued to be retaliatory vengeance for clerical political activities, although this is still one of the major causes. New classes and leaders primarily interested in social and economic reform began to emerge. They attacked the Church, a conservative institution always identified with privilege and vested interests, because it was regarded as an obstacle to social and economic progress. There was new appreciation that the ecclesiastical situation and Church-state relationships were antiquated, reactionary, and out of tune with modern conditions. Well-founded principles, and not merely partisan prejudice underlay the new anti-clerical assault. Leaders like Juárez in Mexico, and [José Manuel] Balmaceda in Chile [president of the republic, 1886-1891], formulated programs and inspired followings. In later days, therefore, anticlericalism in Latin America became, to a certain degree, a political philosophy and plan of action pointing the way to the modern world as the goal.

Americans are often puzzled to find the Church in admittedly Catholic countries subjected to more restrictive legislation than even in Protestant lands. The questions arise: Why is it necessary to hedge the Church by such restrictions? and, Why do the Catholics who constitute the majority tolerate such measures? The first question has already been answered. But, to repeat, the habit of the clergy of meddling in politics and assuming an inordinate supervision over the lives of their parishioners make restrictions necessary. The clergy of Latin America are totally different from the priesthood in the United States. This fact must be born in mind if the Latin American religious situation is to be understood.

As for the second question, it is indeed astonishing that an overwhelming Catholic populace should tolerate religious oppression. There were many prophesies in 1926, when the drastic anticlerical legislation was enforced in Mexico, that there would be a popular uprising. It is true that isolated revolts took place but a general uprising failed to materialize. One could reasonably expect that if the Latin Americans are as devoted to the faith as they are supposed to be, the antireligious laws would be impossible of enforcement. The writer takes no stock in the argument that the people do not revolt since they understand that the reforms are directed at the Church in its temporal aspects and not at the Church as a religion. Undeveloped intellects are incapable of appreciating such fine distinctions. The most loyal Catholics are to be numbered among the women and the members of the lowest classes—those least capable of offering opposition to the government's edicts. Most of the men of the higher classes are "nominal" Catholics, that is, they abstain from contact with the sacraments until the time for the ministration of extreme unction. These men would not fight to the death for the faith. It should be noted, furthermore, that the lowest classes, principally Indians, entertain a profound respect for authority; obedience to superior will has been taught them for centuries, and therefore they would not be apt to oppose the will of the officials —particularly when they are backed by the power of the army. Thus it comes about that in Catholic countries the religion of the majority can be persecuted.

Several of the Latin American countries have, by adhering to wise and tolerant action, attained in separation a satisfactory solution of the vexing religious problem. But in other nations the people are not prepared for the radical change, and therefore they must not be hurried. Their rulers must exercise restraint and make the transition as gradual as possible. On the other hand the Catholic Church should put no obstacle in the way of this change. It should recognize that the modern world is committed to the idea that the ideal status is a free Church in a free state. Adherence to the old pretensions will lead to bitter disputes with inevitable anticlerical attacks and consequent weakening of the hold of the clergy upon the faithful. Recognition of the new order and accommodation to the changed world by a complete severance of Church-state relations, will lead to an active and prosperous Church, which can enjoy the confidence and love of its communicants.

· III ·

THE

Contemporary Scene

※

A Pastoral Letter on
Catholic Social Justice and
the Struggle Against Communism

The Guatemalan revolution of 1944 that overthrew
long-term dictator Jorge Ubico championed political,
economic, and social reform. Originally, the movement
seemed to be under the control of noncommunist, but
anticlerical and secularist leaders. Conservative spokesmen and many churchmen began almost at once to
brand the revolution as communist. By 1954 communists had indeed succeeded in gaining considerable
influence, if not actual control, over the Guatemalan
administration. At this time, Archbishop Mariano Rossell y Arellano spoke out boldly against the communist
menace. Such criticism entailed risk, for the constitution then in effect stipulated that churchmen could
not publicly express political opinions. The archbishop
blamed the advent of communism on the lack of social
justice in Guatemala. In insisting that the Church
alone has an acceptable body of social teachings he was
only stressing the long-established position of the
Catholic faith. Thus, Pope Leo XIII stated: "No practical solution of the question of social matters will be
found apart from the counsel of religion and of the

From *Carta Pastoral del Arzobispo Monseñor Mariano Rossell y
Arellano*, April 4, 1954.

Church"; *while Pope Pius XI averred: "The Church enjoys the indisputable competence to decide whether the bases of a given system are in accord with the unchangeable order which God our Creator and Redeemer has shown us through the Natural Law and Revelation."*

VENERABLE brethren and dearly beloved sons. The bishops were appointed by God Our Lord to safeguard the integrity of the Christian doctrine among those who have been entrusted to their care, and to defend their flocks against the attacks of enemies, whether they come overtly or as wolves concealed in sheep's clothing. Throughout the history of the Church, then, we see that wherever heresy appeared and whenever dangerous doctrines against morals or against any of the rights of God or of His Church have threatened to subvert the faithful, the bishops have spoken out with clear voice. For the bishops have no one to obey in their pastoral duties other than God Our Lord and His Vicar on earth. The bishops must exercise their rights even if this subjects them to the most terrible of martyrdoms, the assassination of the personality, a fate that has been suffered by our beloved and admired Cardinal Mindszenty and by many other bishops and flocks behind the Iron Curtain that are today suffering the worst persecution the Church has ever endured.

For this reason, we must once again call to the attention of the Catholics, and alert them against, the worst of the atheistic doctrines: anti-Christian communism, which today is impudently invading our country. It attempts to infiltrate among us by demanding the economic and social recovery of the poorest classes. It calls for the peasants and workers to add their efforts to its destructive campaign so that tomorrow it can enslave them and subject them to still harsher labor conditions and to the very worst of miseries. This is the nature of communism. To rule, it must divide. And those who help it today will be put to death tomorrow. Thus has it been since the dark and tragic history of communist

Russia began, the country that has murdered the largest number of peasants and workers in the entire history of the world.

In a joint letter of 1946, all the bishops of Guatemala raised their voices in unison to express alarm over the presence of communism at the very doors of our country. But our warning went unheeded, and while the doors of this country were being closed to the ministers of the Catholic faith, to priests and religious, they were being opened wide to a mob of international adventurers quite well trained in communist techniques, and under the discipline of the Third International. In violation of Guatemalan laws, complete freedom was accorded those whose fundamental goal was the overthrow of the government and the de-Christianization of the human soul. They initiated a fierce campaign against national unity. Their efforts led to deep division, irreconcilable anger, and hatred among the workers, some of whom, consistent with this regrettable doctrine, chose to obey Moscow, while others remained first and foremost Guatemalans and Catholics. The government's radio stations began constantly to broadcast speeches of subversive indoctrination, attacks against the Church and its ministers, and proclamations filled with all of the political slogans of the Soviet Politburo. Newsstands began to display communist literature. Even in the schools, the classrooms became centers of communist indoctrination administered by mercenary teachers. While all of this was taking place, the communist cells were active and growing. Witnessing these outrages against the dignity of the Catholic Guatemalan people, the shepherd of our flock did not cease to urge his people to fight and oppose communist tactics. He explained that in accordance with the principles of our sacrosanct religion, Pius IX in 1846 had categorically condemned atheistic communism, and its ridiculous, shameful puppet, socialism. In more recent years communism was once more condemned by Pius XII.

Again, dear brethren, I must talk to all of you, so that you may know with greater certainty what this communism is, against which the spirit of the decent people of Guatemala is aroused. The words of your shepherd are meant to lead Catholics toward a just, national, and dignified campaign against communism. The people of Guatemala must arise as one man to fight the enemy of God and of their country. Our fight against communism, therefore, must be based upon a nationalistic and a Catholic attitude. Let us undertake the campaign against communism in the name of God, and with God, but never animated by petty political interests.

In communism there inheres the notion of a false redemption. It promises the peasants, the workers, and the poor in general to distribute among them the now unequally divided wealth of this world. It asks the proletariat to believe that the only goods are material ones, that religion is futile and unnecessary because there is no God, that religion is in fact the opiate of the people; that children are subject not to the authority of their parents but to the state; that the husband has no obligations toward his wife; that women can and should indulge in unrestricted free love; that there is only one god, the state, in whose behalf children should give up their parents and parents their children; that all forms of faith in God are ridiculous and contrary to the interests of the state. In short, the Soviet paradise is a concentration camp where everyone is forced to work for the state by means of tanks and cannons!

Communist propaganda has penetrated to the farthest corners of Guatemala and has sown its fatal seed in many places, where it has been nourished by the blood of our Guatemalan brothers. What can eradicate this seed in our country? Only the grace of our omnipotent God. Catholics everywhere, by utilizing all means available to them as free human beings in a hemisphere not yet enslaved by the Soviet dictatorship, enjoying the sacred freedom that is theirs as sons of God, must fight and counterattack that doctrine which is opposed to God and to Guatemala. For communism is atheism and atheism is antipatriotic.

Communism is extremely astute, and its tactics are remarkably diverse. It employs all kinds of devices to gain adherents. Communists even dare to pose as good Catholics in order to win the confidence of our people. Communists, who by their very nature spread discord and division, have the temerity to organize peace campaigns. They hope thus to distract the rest of the world while secretly, day and night, they work to manufacture the implements of war. They take advantage of disagreements between workers and management, of the divisions among families. They create anarchy in countries, and always their only goal is the seizure of power. To aid them in this purpose they make promises to the peasants and workers, promises that are never fulfilled.

There is not a single code of justice that will counsel us to search for peace with a powerful country that has enslaved millions of human beings and intends to erase completely from the face of the earth the very name of God and the dignity of mankind!

Communism takes advantage of the prevailing economic inequality to seduce those who have nothing. Communism furtively resorts to measures to make food shortages more acute so as to increase discontent among the poor and to make them believe that only through communism can they emerge from their painful circumstances.

The Church has always proclaimed that the right to own property is a natural and inalienable right. At the same time, by condemning superfluous luxuries, ostentation, and wastefulness it has proscribed the excessive ownership of goods by a small, greedy minority. For centuries, the Church has asked nations to bring about a more equitable distribution of wealth. Many years ago the Church spoke out on the salaries of workers, and stated that remuneration for labor should not be so limited as to provide only for personal, individual needs, but should be sufficient to meet family expenses. Over a century ago it addressed itself to the rich, the selfishly wealthy and powerful sectors and, by way of serious reproach, prophesied their responsibility for bringing about the rise of that very communism which today infests our world.

In its social formulas the Church goes farther than any other organization that has sought to solve the problems of the misery of the working class. Precisely because the Church has defended the rights of the workers against the powerful wealthy, communism fears it more than the combined armed forces of all governments. History proves that communism has been able to prevail in countries boasting great military traditions and enjoying genuine military power, precisely by overcoming that armed might. But communism has never been able to further its conquests where Catholic social teachings were accepted! The best way to assist communist infiltration is to make it impossible for the Church to preach its social doctrines. Historically, the social teachings and actions of the Church have always been the anticommunist dike. For this reason, my dear Guatemalan brethren, I fully trust you, wherever the voice of the Church can still reach you and bring to you this anguished message of alert at a time when there is no country in the world free from the communist virus. I trust because I know that our people are still genuinely Catholic in their traditions. Above all, I trust God and His Divine Providence, alive in each page of our history yesterday and today, God Who cannot exempt me from the duty I have to summon one and all to fight communism with the most effective weapons we have: *social justice* and Christian charity.

In the matter of social justice, the Church is ever consistent in favoring the proletariat. For centuries it has preached to the wealthy to impress upon them not only their obligations to help those who have nothing, but also their responsibilities of social justice. As championed by the Church, social justice demands from individuals all that is necessary to bring about the common good. We join our voice with that of Pius XI in saying:

The demands of social justice are not satisfied if we permit workers to continue to live without the secure enjoyment of what is required for their personal support and for that of their families, without a salary duly proportional to meet these needs; if we do not make possible the acquisition by workers of modest material comfort so as to bring an end to the plague of universal poverty; if we do not see that by public and private social security measures they can enjoy the conveniences of health and unemployment insurance and old-age pensions. (*Divini Redemptoris*)

To provide the worker with whatever is demanded by social justice will be to render remote the possibility of a communist conquest. Therefore, the worker must come to know that the Church offers him a just and generous plan, a program of genuine social recovery that differs, as the light from darkness, from the glittering one with which the communists attempt to deceive him.

The Church believes in the just right of the association of the economically weak, of the proletariat, in order that they may contend with their exploiters. But it will always try to prevent these organizations from falling under the domination of communists, Marxists, pure secularists, or persons suspected of such ideologies!

To lighten the burden of misery and the inequality of wealth that will always exist in the world as a consequence of original sin, the Church has steadfastly taught Christian charity. This it has taught not as a mere devotion or as a pious practice, but as a moral obligation. Christian charity has the power to accomplish what social justice alone can never attain. It can alleviate the suffering of and extend help to the needy when they are oppressed by adverse circumstances. Let us not forget that Christ tells us in the Gospels that acts of Christian charity will open for us the gates of Heaven.

Christian charity, always together with social justice, are the best means to fight atheistic communism and its fatal infiltration of the poorest classes.

Our Lord in the Holy Eucharist Who has witnessed in our recent Eucharistic Congresses the greatest acts of homage that Guatemala has ever rendered in its entire history, will be Our Leader in this National Crusade against communism. This crusade will be one of sacrifices and prayers as well as of intense efforts to spread the social doctrines of the Church and to refute communist propaganda. And all of this will be inspired by love of God and of Guatemala.

JUAN DOMINGO PERON

A Denunciation of Certain Argentine Churchmen

In exercising the right it claims as the supreme teacher in matters of social justice, the Church can come into conflict with ideologies other than atheistic communism. As the philosophical basis for his broad social and economic program, Juan Domingo Perón (president of Argentina, 1946-1955) and his partisans concocted justicialismo, a body of thought which allegedly contained the formula for creating a perfect balance between individualism and collectivism, materialism and idealism. Justicialismo lacked any direct Christian or Catholic orientation. It was regarded by clergymen as purely secular and pragmatic. Alarmed by this, and by Perón's program of social reform, which acknowledged no connection with Catholic teachings and which was winning enthusiastic response among the lower classes, certain clergymen, working largely through lay Catholic Action groups, began to assume a role in labor and professional organizations. One of their purposes was to initiate a social-reform movement that would be under the influence of the Church. Probably fearing that a rival political party could emerge from this movement, Perón began a heated attack.

From the November 10, 1954 address of Perón to an assembly of provincial and territorial governors and representatives of provincial labor organizations, printed in the now defunct *Hechos E Ideas*—Buenos Aires—, XXVII, Nos. 126-127 (October-November, 1954), excerpts from pp. 387-397.

THE organization "Catholic Action of Argentina," which is international in character, includes among its members certain anti-Peronists. In fact, the anti-Peronists control this organization. They act with suave hypocrisy. It is their custom to attend meetings and to talk like this: "I do not come here in the name of Catholic Action. . . ." Yet, in reality, they are operating in its name. We must subject this type of Catholic Action member to our careful scrutiny. It is often the same with the clergy. What is the clergy? An organization, like any other, where we may find good people, bad people, and very bad people. I have never heard of an organization of men in which every single one was good. This would indeed be an extraordinary case. In all organizations there are always many bad members, and in all justice this fact must be acknowledged. So, there are bad members among the clergy, and there are Peronists and anti-Peronists as well. This is no secret. All that is necessary is that we know how to distinguish between these men, and that we treat the Peronists as Peronists, and the anti-Peronists as anti-Peronists.

This has nothing to do with the Church in itself, and I want to make this point quite clear. I have talked with high dignitaries of the Church, with bishops and archbishops, who are simply men like any of the rest of us. I presented to them the problems now being encountered by those organizations that are suffering injury because of the attitudes of several Catholic groups. And I confronted the prelates in the presence of the representatives of those organizations that are being injured. I had received urgent notice that restlessness was mounting not only in the small syndicates but also in the General Confederation of Labor, in the Confederation of Professionals, in the General Confederation of University Students, in other student organizations, and in many other groups. So, I told the prelates:

I do not understand why they are being organized, these groups of Catholic laborers, Catholic lawyers, Catholic doctors, and Catholic farmers. We are Catholics too! But to be Peronists we do not have to proclaim that we are Catholic Peronists. We are simply Peronists, and within this context we can be Catholic, Jewish, Buddhist, Orthodox, or what have you. It is not necessary for us to ask a Peronist which God he prays to. For us, the faith that a person professes is irrelevant, so long as the person is a good human being. That is all that counts!

The prelates agreed with us, and before all those representatives of the victimized organizations who were present as witnesses, they—the bishops and archbishops —were the first to condemn those priests who were not faithful to their duties. They added that they not only condemned such men, but declared them enemies against the ecclesiastical dignity. This was said by the prelates, and certainly I ought to honor and place credence in the voice of the prelates!

If those who have the responsibility for the welfare of the Church in Argentina, in the presence of the members of various interested organizations, state with the solemnity always accompanying a declaration made before the first magistrate of the republic that they condemn those priests and those Catholics who disturb the public order, we ought to honor their voice. And because we do honor it, we expect the prelates to keep their word when the government, or organizations of the state, or of the people, begin to carry out the necessary measures against those few prelates who are not only opposed to the government of the nation but also to the Church, and who are thereby declared enemies against the ecclesiastical dignity of the republic of Argentina.

Our government cannot believe, and our program of political action cannot be based upon the belief, that this statement could have been made only to meet a given situation, and that it was a lie! I trust the word of those men who represent the Church in Argentina. And consequently, we must take appropriate measures when we encounter men who have failed to fulfill their duties as Argentine citizens and as priests. They are operating beyond the laws of their country, and beyond the laws of God as well. Therefore, we know already what we are going to do with them. There is no law of the republic that will prevent us from taking measures against any citizen, of any profession whatsoever, when he acts in manner contrary to good customs and is guilty of transgressing the laws of the republic. Those who act in this fashion will be punished according to the law. But all of this pertains only to individuals. The Church itself is not involved in these matters, as is clear from the fact that its very leaders condemn those priests who fail to fulfill their duties, both as Argentines and as priests!

For us the situation is absolutely clear. It belongs to us, as civil authorities, to see that these men fulfill their duties at least to the state. The prelates will provide for taking the necessary means to make them fulfill their religious duties, and this problem is no concern of ours.

So far as the action of various organizations is concerned, we shall proceed in similar fashion. If the prelates have condemned the priests who do not meet their obligations, they must also condemn the organizations established to interfere with and disrupt governmental action. We have the legal means to respond with all necessary measures in this situation. Any organization that cannot licitly obtain the goals of its program, be they announced or covert, ought to be immediately suppressed, and its leaders subjected to the appropriate processes. No matter under what label they operate, they must be condemned for illicit action if they participate in an illicit association. From now on all those associations that function ostensibly for one purpose, and actually try to achieve a different one, must be considered illicit, and therefore subject to intervention by the civil authority. The law does not allow social organizations committed overtly to one purpose to pursue furtively a different one. If organizations are legal and legitimate, and consequently enjoy the right of carrying on a given activity, they should limit themselves to this activity. If they interfere in the legal activities of other associations, they should immediately be abolished and prosecuted, according to the law, as illicit organizations.

We have all of the necessary means at our disposal. It is only a question of using them in a manner that will be in accordance with our concern for the well-being of the Church, which we are now trying to encourage to cleanse itself of those men who have arisen against its authority.

Córdoba, unquestionably, is the place where the most unusual occurrences have taken place. There, one encounters a certain Father Bordagaray, associated with the University of Córdoba, who says that we have to make a choice between Christ and Perón. I have never had a conflict with Christ. Precisely what I am trying to do is defend the doctrines of Christ, which for over two hundred years priests of this type in Argentina have sought unsuccessfully to destroy.

I also believe that a certain Father José V. López, a Spaniard, is in Córdoba. We are about to take the necessary measures against him. There also is Father Julio Treviño, who claims that we are promoting delinquency by having swimming pools in the jails. I do not know what this has to do with Christian piety, but I do know that it has a great deal to do with sanitation. Whether or not this priest bathes in the swimming pool does not concern me.

For us, this is simply a matter of individuals. There are approximately 16,000 members of the clergy here. We will not raise a problem with the Church because twenty or thirty among them are opponents. It is natural that among such a large number there should be some who are against us. What must we do? Simply take measures against those few. The hierarchy is eminently correct when it tells me that the matter does not pertain to the Church, but only to some of its misguided priests. We are going to help the Church put them in their proper place. That is all!

Peronism and the Intensified Attack
Against the Church

Argentine churchmen in 1955, probably much to the surprise of their critics, came close to presenting a common front against the claims of Peronism. Rejecting Perón's contention that the disputed issue was one between representatives of the people and a few clergymen, Church leaders maintained that moral questions and the basic philosophy of social justice were involved. In both instances, the Church reserved the right to speak out and to demand respect for its voice. On June 16, 1955, there occurred an abortive uprising against Perón. Churchmen were widely blamed by Peronists for having instigated the insurrection. An editorial in Hechos E Ideas, an organ of Peronism, noted that a central point in the continuing dispute was the right claimed by the Church to exercise influence in the sphere of social justice. Charging the Church with a past record of callous neglect of the social question, the journal implied that social justice was the exclusive sphere of the government. It also implied that any matter on which the federal government passed legislation thereby became purely political in nature and consequently beyond the competence of the Church.

THE unsuccessful revolutionary attempt of June 16th raises a serious question concerning the growth and development of our incipient democratic institutions. In

From *Hechos E Ideas*, XXVII, Nos. 134-135 (June-July), 1955, excerpts from pp. 481-491.

fact, it raises a doubt about the survival of government of the people, by the people, and for the people, to use the well-known expression of Lincoln. An impartial analysis of the recent events leads one to make this most serious observation.

The insurrection instigated by reactionary elements shows quite clearly the extremes of barbarian procedures to which the "select clerical minorities" would resort if ever they gained power by violence—the only manner in which they could come to power. This frustrated attempt should reawaken a sense of reality among all sincere democrats and defenders of public freedom who, because of various rivalries and political tensions, have connived with the insurgents whose secret and despicable dream is a revival of the dark past that can never come to life again. This is not a capricious affirmation. Its truth arises from the fact that history cannot be reversed. Revolutionary endeavors to overthrow the legally established authorities are puny expedients resorted to by a powerful minority that does not wish to accept the will of the majority. The minority rejects the majority as inferior, imbued with unhealthy passions, stupid, and intolerant. In reality, stupidity and intolerance, together with highly developed sadism and cruelty, have always been the typical attributes of the "select clerical minorities" whose reactionary spirit has led to their loss of all sense of morality.

Little did these people care about the hundreds of innocent victims murdered by the grapeshot during that day of infamy. Instead, they reacted with pious manifestations of faith and of indignation—daring and provoking ostentation patiently tolerated by the government—to the sacrilege perpetrated by the inflamed crowds that burned down three or four churches. We do not approve of the misbehavior involved in church arson. But we justify it because we consider the Church and clericalism to have been responsible for the events of June 16th! Moreover, we justify this misbehavior because we consider the Church and clericalism to have instigated a violent reaction against the will of the majority in the nation and against its very government. This government will not tolerate their interference in social, political, and economic decisions that belong exclusively, according to our constitution, to the civil power.

This ill-advised campaign was begun furtively by organized elements of Catholic Action which sought to undermine union organizations by establishing so-called Catholic labor unions. The only conceivable goal of these Catholic unions was the destruction of existing worker organizations. The campaign then developed new methods. To put it clearly, it utilized the support of the clergy.

Clericalism and the Church, or to put it more exactly Argentine clericalism and the Church of Argentina, did not look happily upon the work that the government was carrying out in several aspects of its cultural program. Consequently, the battle began in the churches, where the Sunday sermons were used to broadcast Catholic criticism of the work of the government! The Church, which by one of those incredible concessions of the Perón revolution had achieved the reinstitution of religious instruction in the schools, was beginning to reveal its pretensions and true intentions! It was now pretending to teach rules of conduct to the government!

As was bound to happen, the Argentine parliament suppressed religious instruction in public schools, reestablishing laic education. It also passed other laws, such as the one permitting divorce, which had previously been prevented from becoming a part of our legislative structure by clerical prejudices.

These laws passed by parliament, and consequently representing the will of the government, provoked a tremendous reaction from the Church. Elements of the displaced oligarchy and all the other opposition forces could not let pass this excellent opportunity to foment artificial commotion. They joined in the Church campaign. Other elements joined also, among them even some men who had been benefited by the nation-

alistic, Perón revolution—the authentic embodiment
of the sovereignty of the people, a government with
powers conferred by consecutive elections, honest and
decent as never before in the past! The clerical "conglomeration" included even a small number of Marine
and Air Force officers, transformed into self-styled sav-
iors of the country and protectors of the people—of the
very people whom they cowardly murdered. And finally
the conglomeration included a few "virtuous national-
ists," whom we think deserving of special mention.
They engaged in a secret propaganda campaign among
the armed forces, denouncing the government for having betrayed our national oil interests and resorting to
a suspicious sort of Jacobinism. Clerical planning provided the unifying force for this motley coalition. The
notion was to use this coalition to carry out the nefarious, criminal work of clericalism, that was to begin by
murdering the president of the republic and to end,
after a series of vindictive atrocities, by implanting a
fascistic dictatorship under the motto, "Order, Country, and Freedom."

No possible doubt can remain as to the role of the
Church in the disruption of public order. By their concrete actions the clergy and members of Catholic Action flaunted the standing regulations forbidding public
manifestations and disobeyed the rules both of the Minister of the Interior and of Police which had been formulated to preserve internal peace and public security.
A proof of clerical insubordination is the July 18th
"Declaration" of the bishops. It reveals their opposition to any restriction of their freedom and criticizes
the laws of the country and various resolutions of the
civil power. We admit that the Church should defend
its interests, which is all that it does defend, and so bitterly at that. But it seems to us absolutely intolerable
that it should pretend to teach norms of conduct to
the civil power. Likewise, we consider irresponsible and
reprehensible the attempt of Catholics and of all our
other political enemies to intimidate the electorate of
the country and public opinion with the threat of an

oligarchical-fascist-clerical counterrevolution that will provoke civil war.

From these events one may infer that there are people who think the problems of our incipient democracy must be solved by the violent removal of the government of the majority. Impatient politicians, goaded on by personal ambition, are unwilling to tolerate transitory flaws, that can actually best be mended by continuing to expand the base of political participation. If men like this are to have their way, then we shall have gone back to the times of obscurantism and the Inquisition, in other words, to barbarian times, when problems were solved through processes of mutual destruction!

At the present time, all the bishops of the republic, whose respective dioceses are supported by the state, have denounced that very state and in their previously mentioned "Declaration" have denounced as "religious persecution" acts that are legitimate attributes of the civil power. They have denounced the suppression of the Agency of the General Administration and Supervision of Religious Instruction, the law concerning public meetings, the law providing for absolute divorce, the law of social prophylaxis, the suppression of religious feast days, the removal of religious instruction, the removal of tax exemption on the tremendous wealth of the Church and its institutions, and finally the law that calls for an assembly to make reforms in the constitution regarding those articles that deal with the Catholic cult and to consider the separation of Church and state. From this we can infer that the civil power has no right to restrict any of the fabulous privileges of the Church, and that, on the other hand, the Church is ready to make the government respond to its authority as an ecclesiastical power. This is proved by various aspects of the "Declaration," in which the Church reveals its pride and arrogance. As an example of this, we can quote certain passages. "The bishops did not demand from the [Perón] revolution the reinstitution of religious instruction in the school system; rather, the Catholics

themselves who joined the revolution demanded it."
Concerning the suppression of religious feast days, the
"Declaration" observes: "This lack of respect for the
Holy See, with which it would have been possible to
come to an agreement, will always be regrettable."

In the first instance, pertaining to the matter of religious instruction, we call attention to the arrogance of
the bishops who signed the "Declaration." In the second, regarding religious feast days, we can readily observe the opinion of the Argentine Church concerning
the sovereignty of the state. In both cases, episcopal
contempt for the government of the people is clear.

Another aspect of the "Declaration" to which we
wish to call attention is the following:

The same press accused the Church—with the insults and
diatribes well known to this country—of having failed in
its social mission by not working to carry out social reforms. It accuses the Church of an alliance with the
wealthy. Then, in most illogical fashion, it warns the
Church to seclude itself within the temples and to confine its activities exclusively to the spiritual realm! We are
convinced that social reform requires a basic doctrinal
foundation and that no doctrine or methods alien to the
Catholic doctrine and Catholic moral teachings can ever
supply such a foundation. In making this statement we
come to the most serious part of our documentation that
proves our justification in denouncing the persecution of
the Church in the republic of Argentina.

As we can see, this statement has overlooked nothing.
Just what have been the tangible evidences that the
Church has fulfilled its social mission? The diatribes
and insults of the press, accusing it of having gone
hand in hand with the oligarchy and of having formed
an alliance with the wealthy, might displease it. But
such affirmations are not insults or diatribes. They are
true and irrefutable statements of fact. When, and in
what way, has the Church done social work in our
country? Or, to ask this question in another way, what
have been the indications of its interest in bettering
the standard of living of the poor classes while they

suffered from the worst forms of exploitation without legal protection of any kind? The attitude of the Church toward the glaring social inequalities that the masses had to endure was one of indifference. The poor classes never concerned it. The Church does not support itself or increase its wealth by concerning itself over so unproductive a flock. Money? yes, that interests it. And money is the possession of the wealthy.

For those who have already lived a little and who already know how things go with the Argentine Church, it will not be difficult to recall the case of Monsignor Miguel de Andrea. When he was promoted to the post of archbishop of Buenos Aires, he was quickly replaced by Father Bottaro. And then Monsignor Copello was named archbishop of Buenos Aires. This brought an end to the social work that Miguel de Andrea, and not the Church, had been doing in his own way. The House of Catholic Working Women, and the Bathing Resort of Catholic Working Women at Mar del Plata stand as evidences of the social work of Monsignor de Andrea. These were huge possessions which we suppose are today being utilized for the economic gain of the Church! At any rate, when Monsignor de Andrea was appointed archbishop of Buenos Aires the Jesuits began such a powerful campaign against him that Rome had to stop the appointment. The beneficiary of this curious campaign, that reveals some of the *subrosa* dealings of the Church of Argentina, was Monsignor Copello, designated at the end as archbishop of Buenos Aires. The naming of Bottaro was just a coverup step, and shortly he had to resign as his poor health did not allow him to administer the affairs of the archbishopric.

It would have been better for the prelates not to mention the "social work of the Church" that today the government of the people "does not permit it to carry out!"

Finally, the Church of Argentina, which does not interfere in politics as does the oligarchy and the political parties opposed to the government, points out [in the "Declaration"] "the urgent need to reestablish the indispensable conditions that will make possible the free and complete expression of a genuine and true opinion corresponding to the thought and will of the country." And it adds:

In order to achieve this, it is absolutely necessary to have freedom of assembly, of press, and of radio, unobstructed by direct or indirect restrictions. Only with such freedom can legitimate public opinion express itself. We consider as an urgent need the due protection of the rights and legitimate freedom of the Church and of institutions, of the rights of public freedom and of the human person, so that tranquility and order, which inhere in peace, may restore the confidence and stability desired by everyone.

The Church, as the Radical and other political parties of the opposition, forgets that even though it is true that the government has had to restrict the freedom of the press and public opinion in order to attain the goals proposed by the revolution—as General Perón has explained—the government is still the authentic representative of the popular will. The elections of February 24, 1946 that brought Perón to the presidency of the nation followed all of the prescribed rules for democratic elections; Perón was repudiated by the combined forces of the clergy,* the socialists and communists, the Progressive Democrats, the Radicals and Conservatives, the Argentine Industrial Union, the stock exchange, the big capitalist corporations both national and foreign, the imperialists, and the like, all led by the notorious Mr. Spruille Braden, Ambassador of the United States. The entire press of the nation supported this incredible coalition to fight the "impossible candidate," as they used to call Perón, predicting only insignificant electoral support for him.

The Church and all the forces opposed to Perón will be able to act with entire freedom and with full guarantees in the electoral campaign that will precede the elections for the national convention that will consider

---

* The introduction to this book takes exception to this statement.

modification of the constitution. Before this campaign begins Perón will declare the revolution ended because it has accomplished its fundamental goals, and will restore to all the populace the famous individual guarantees that were previously the exclusive possession of the minorities. The people, in this crisis, will decide whether or not the Church will be separated from the state. The Church should contain its passion and gather its strength for this electoral campaign, rather than using its might in the present circumstances to attempt to overthrow Perón by violence. The Church knows that what has lately transpired has been "to the greater glory of God," even though its bad shepherds may not see it that way!

Catholic Social Justice,

Authoritarianism,

and Class Stratification

In the following selection, Jorge Iván Hübner Gallo, a leading spokesman of conservatism in Chile, as well as an influential, young professor at the national university, explains his opposition to the Catholic liberalism advocated by his country's Christian Democratic Party. Although Hübner asserts that the frequent refusal of Christian Democrats to voice sweeping and blanket condemnations of communism is in opposition to Church teaching, it is worth noting the words, in 1961, of Chilean Bishop Bernardo Pinera of Temuco: "If bishops or priests forthrightly condemn the communists who seemingly are trying to help the poor, the workers will distrust them and bracket them along with the rich classes and the impersonal rich countries like the United States." Hübner's principal contention is that social justice must be administered paternalistically, within a stratified, closed society. He envisions the corporate state, allegedly the system of the middle ages, as a means for achieving this type of social structure. The corporate state signifies to him one in which people are represented in the national legislature not according to numbers, but according to their occupations or functions. Each functional-interest group

From Jorge Iván Hübner Gallo, *Los católicos en la política* (Santiago de Chile, 1959), excerpts from pp. 65-96. By permission of Empresa Editora Zig-Zag, S.A., Santiago de Chile.

should select a prescribed number of delegates to the national congress. In selecting these delegates, the small number of employers in each group should have equal voice with the masses of employees. Men of capital and property would thus be benefited by a weighted vote.

THE National Falange in Chile [forerunner of the Christian Democratic Party], like the Christian leftist groups in France, has its deep ideological roots in the revolutionary romanticism of the eighteenth century, which dogmatically proclaimed the natural goodness of man and glorified the concept of popular sovereignty based on liberty, equality, and fraternity. The vain attempts of Felicité Robert de Lamennais in the past century and of Marc Sangnier in the present to reconcile these romantic concepts with Christianity also influenced the incipient Falange, as did the Marxian analysis of the importance of the proletariat, the class struggle, the economic factors in society, and the weaknesses of the capitalist system which were supposed inevitably to prepare the way for socialism.

These doctrinal streams were channeled into one riverbed and filtered in recent decades by the French Catholic philosopher, Jacques Maritain. Later, the resulting ideology was carried into practice on the level of public administration by the popular republican movement in France. In this body of thought the Catholic youth of Chile, lacking both adequate training and experience, found first a new intellectual master, and afterwards a model for political action.

The founders of the National Falange read Maritain avidly and followed with unbounded admiration the newest tendencies of French Catholicism. They attacked the capitalist system outspokenly and saw communism more as the embodiment of an aspiration for social justice than as a threat of destruction to the Christian world. No one is unaware of the fact that they aligned with Maritain on the Spanish question, favoring the nefarious red republic and attacking the national and Catholic movement led by General Francisco Franco.

Until 1938 this handful of young Chilean idealists, although disoriented, remained within the confines of a Catholic confessional political party. They remained, in short, within the Conservative Party. Gradually, though, this advanced guard within the Conservative Party began to exhibit a vague spirit of rebellion against traditional standards. Little by little the future founders of the Falange adopted a new position within the Conservative Party. They were the least in number and the youngest, but they wanted to impose their criteria upon the entire party. What constituted their "advanced" program? Neither at that time nor subsequently have they been able to formulate a concrete plan of action, nor to develop a concrete program of dissent from the traditional views of the Conservative Party on economic and social questions.

The Christian Democrats in Chile, like their counterparts in France, began by professing a true idolatry of democracy, liberty, and human rights, inspired directly by secularist liberalism. They do not try to temper majoritarian democracy in any fashion so as to render it legitimate and acceptable. They think of the rights of the individual rather than of the common good. They do not contemplate organizing suffrage upon a logical, hierarchical basis, but are content to rest it upon a foundation of equalitarianism; nor are they willing to place upon liberty the restraints demanded in the interest of moral goodness and truth. Their ideology rests neither upon the glorious Aristotelian-Thomistic tradition, nor upon pontifical teachings. Instead, it is rooted in the liberalism of the French Revolution, poorly disguised by the varnish of Christianity concocted by the philosophical talent of Maritain.

The Falange rejects the ideals of the Catholic state as anachronistic and totalitarian, and wishes to have nothing to do with a frankly confessional system like that of Franco's Spain today. On the other hand, it affirms the necessity of building a profane society, fraternal and pluralistic, in which all ideologies and creeds will coexist in harmony, and in which the Catholic Church will enjoy no special consideration. This idolatry of democracy has led, in effect, to an enthusiastic espousal of universal suffrage, and to an insistence upon the unconditional right of any person publicly to express any faith or idea. This, in essence, explains why the Falange opposes any "repressive" measure in restraint of the civic "rights" or the freedom of organization and expression of the Communist Party. The communist agents, as "persons," should enjoy, according to this naïve and tolerant liberal outlook, exactly the same guarantees as well-ordered and conscientious elements in society. Moreover, manifesting in this regard the influence of Rousseau's anthropology, the Falangists believe with a candid optimism that in the free discussion of all ideas, communism will be defeated dialectically and that the truth will assert itself.

Those who formulated this body of theories forget that authority comes from God and that the state has the obligation to render respect officially to the Supreme Being. They forget also that political society has not only temporal ends but also objectives pertaining to the spiritual good of society; and they forget that the individual, weakened by original sin, tends often toward error and evil. Thus, there corresponds to the public authority the duty to hinder the diffusion of creeds and ideas contrary to truth.

Democracy, far from being an end in itself, is only one of the many systems of government which could be adopted as a means of obtaining the common good, and it is only legitimate if it adjusts itself to the demands of the natural law and the Christian conscience. The Falange desires not a Catholic state but a liberal democracy of the type advocated by Rousseau. It is enough to read its political literature to be convinced of this.

Because of the nonconformist impulse of its founders, the Falange arose from within the innermost recesses of conservatism. From the very moment the movement saw the light of day, it felt it essential to demonstrate that, in spite of its origins, it was "advanced, progressive, and unbiased." It was necessary that its position should never, even by coincidence, be in harmony with Conservative policy, no matter how just it might be. Such harmony would inspire doubts among the new friends of the leftist Falange.

Except for its consistent political policy of entering into frequent alliances with the extreme left, the Falange has not demonstrated a program; it is more declamatory than practical. Its leaders attack eloquently the vices of capitalism; but we don't know of any concrete legislative proposals advanced by its congressmen to solve the socio-economic problems of the country. In this regard the Falangist sterility contrasts with the bountiful action of the much maligned Conservative Party, to which the major portion of social legislation promulgated in Chile during the past half century may be attributed. Of course, it is easier to criticize than to construct. But when criticism is made without offering anything in the way of a constructive alternative, it becomes nothing more than deplorable demagoguery.

In its position of academic leftism, the Falange reveals its impregnation by Marxian socialist value judgments. There is no other explanation for the fact that both the Falangists and international communists pay primary attention to economic problems. For the Falangists, the most urgent and pressing consideration is the solution of this type of problem. They are willing to postpone consideration of the religious and spiritual needs of the people. The secularism of their policies is characteristic of the attitudes of leftist Catholics, who object to the traditional values and label them "clerical," who pretend that it is not possible to go back to the *status quo* of the middle ages, and who maintain that religious questions are no longer uppermost and that the state should concern itself only with providing for the material needs of the workers.

It is also typical of the Christian leftism which the Falange professes to picture communism as the product of the misery of the popular classes and to claim that it can be defeated through the improvement of working-class living conditions. This erroneous conception, arising from the excessive importance attached to economic factors, ignores the essential spiritual aspect of the communist heresy and seeks to interpret all social phenomena according to the Marxian dialectic.

Far more than the product of a misdirected aspiration for justice, communism is a terrible and satanic negation of God and of the spirit; it is a total heresy. The evil malignancy of communism cannot be removed from the souls it has infested by economic expedients. The only effective means to accomplish its ouster is the Christian faith, the one path to truth and the good life.

Merely raising the living standards of a people will not protect them from the communist contamination. The leaders of the Soviet sect are never paupers. Usually they are persons who enjoy a comfortable material existence. But this does not lead them to renounce their tainted ideas. Besides, it has been demonstrated more than once that a communist nucleus can begin and flourish in the midst of well-paid workers who enjoy material advantages.

The leftist propensity of the Falange, which has caused its policy to coincide so often with that of the communists, not only reveals itself in the statements of some of its leaders and intellectual mentors, but also in the official Falangist political party line, both domestic and international. As Sergio Fernández Larraín astutely observes in his carefully documented *Falange Nacional, Democracia Cristiano, y Comunismo*, the Falange, although affirming the need to instill the Christian social doctrine in the country,

proceeds then to advocate methods which negate Christian social principles. This is owing primarily to the Falange attitude toward communist activity. Thus, methods aimed at suppressing communism are labeled sterile and inefficient. As a result, Falangists have advocated an approach that actually favors communism and is therefore at variance with true and honest democracy and injurious to the rights of Christian human beings.

This lamentable policy was defended by Senator and Falange leader Eduardo Frei in a talk given on June 27, 1947. "We reject communist doctrine and tactics. *But before communism we see that there is something worse: anticommunism.*"

The Christian Democratic Party has been the main one responsible for the greatest crime committed against the institutional organization of the republic: the abolition in 1958 of Law No. 5,839 concerning the Permanent Defense of Democracy [this law declared the Communist Party illegal].

Not only did the Falange oppose the Law of Permanent Defense of Democracy [when it was proposed and approved in 1948] but also after the law was duly passed it joined forces with the Marxian parties to initiate and maintain a persistent campaign to rescind the law. This campaign, very logical for communists who felt themselves threatened in their anti-national activities but incomprehensible for the members of a party of a democratic and Christian inspiration, was intensified by the formation at the beginning of 1958 of a parliamentary bloc, with the participation of communists and Falangists, one of the principal objectives of which was the abolition of the law.

Because of this development, His Eminence the cardinal-archbishop of Santiago, Monsignor José María Caro, of happy memory, felt it to be his duty to recall, in a public declaration, the norms fixed by the Church concerning the condemnation of communism. Moreover, in the *Revista Católica* in the January-April edition of 1958, the following theological article appeared by Monsignor Alejandro Huneeus Cox, from which I quote a small section:

Do those who vote in favor of the electoral reform, which in part revokes the elimination of communists established by the Law of Permanent Defense of Democracy, directly favor communism and for this reason incur the sanction of being deprived of the sacraments as public sinners? Answered: affirmatively, they do favor it and incur said sanctions.

We must emphasize that Monsignor Huneeus, doctor in theology, holds the position of secretary of the archbishop of Santiago; but he did not write the article in this last capacity, but rather in a private capacity in order to instruct the conscience of the faithful.

All of this did not stop the Christian Democratic congressmen of Chile from taking refuge in the contrary opinions of other ecclesiastical dignitaries. Consequently, by order of the party's directors, they voted in favor of abolishing the Law of Permanent Defense of Democracy, seeking to deliver an irreparable blow against the republican institutions of the country and contributing toward providing the Communist Party with one of the most resounding triumphs it has ever achieved in the Western world.

In international politics, the Falange, in line with its "advanced" position, has also followed a policy in many respects favorable to Soviet imperialism. This is revealed by their attitude toward the important Spanish question.

Spain was the first battlefield on which communist barbarism, represented by the infamous government of the inappropriately named "republic," came face to face with the forces of Western, Christian civilization, represented by the *Alzamiento Nacional* [National Insurrection, of which Franco became the leader]. After the bloody and prolonged fight from 1936 to 1939, during which the Reds carried to unbelievable extremes their crimes and depredations against the Church, the civil war ended in the praiseworthy victory of General Franco, who proceeded to establish on the peninsula a Catholic state that strives to be guided by pontifical teachings and by the glorious political traditions of Castile.

Undoubtedly, Franco's regime is not a liberal democracy in accordance with the taste of Masons and Chilean Falangists. But it does represent an authentic state of law, a bastion of Catholicism where, more than in any other country of the world, there is respect for the dignity of man as a spiritual being and concern for the demands of the common good.

Well then, the directors, the congressmen, and writers of the Chilean National Falange, joining with the anti-Spanish campaign directed from Moscow, have found nothing better to do than to defend the defeated cause of the Reds and to attack Franco's government in virulent manner. On the pretext of upholding the ideals of liberty and democracy, the Chilean Falangists in their attack against Spain are lending and continue to lend immense service to the cause of communist totalitarianism, which receives obvious satisfaction from the spontaneous aid of Catholic leftists.

His Eminence, the late cardinal-archbishop of Santiago, Monsignor José María Caro, in a public declaration of December 11, 1947, specifically censured this Falangist policy. I quote now from a portion of the Cardinal's declaration:

Another matter on which the Falange manifests a judgement in dissonance with that of the Chilean hierarchy, the Pope, and the episcopacy of the entire world that thinks like him and with him, is the Spanish question. We need not go into details. It is enough to know that in this matter we had on one side the activity of a government illegitimate in origin and in the exercise of its power which sought to destroy the religion of the Spanish people, burning its churches and schools, killing bishops, sacking temples, murdering priests and nuns by the thousands and the faithful by the hundreds of thousands. On the other side was the force that stood for the defense of civil and religious liberty and of the patrimony enriched by centuries of Christian civilization.

Well then, we do not know if for love of the democracy which they say is exterminated by the one who freed Spain from the destruction and incredible acts of cruelty to which it had come, or for love of communism, fortunately displaced and prevented from completing its work in the Motherland, the Falangists have shown themselves to be out of accord with the Christian judgement of the world episcopacy, showing instead sympathy for the conquered. If they do it for love of democracy, we are not aware that they have at any time condemned the regimes in those countries like Russia and the satellites where there is not even a hint of democracy.

In that same document, Monsignor Caro lamented that the Falangists had "not mentioned the views of the hierarchy." Instead, they sought counsel from outside the ranks of the episcopacy in regard to matters over which the prelates enjoyed competence. After the cardinal's declaration the National Falange still did not mend its twisted ways. Eleven additional years of mistaken or bungling operations, of destructive leftist politics that have frequently aided Marxian causes, have shown that the Christian Democratic Party of Chile has not known how to understand the severe admonishments of the ecclesiastical hierarchy.

Outside of Spain, always faithful to the traditional doctrine, the nations of the world, some more and others less, are today dominated by governments, by legal structures, and by political systems that are opposed to pontifical teachings. The only possible means to defend Western Christian civilization from the imminent attack of Asiatic barbarism consists in waging the persistent and courageous fight to restore Catholic ideals, represented in civil life by conservative and traditional parties.

On our part, we think that the ideological basis of traditional conservatism is epitomized in three great concepts which together constitute the prerequisite conditions for all progress. All three are rooted in natural reason and natural law. These are the concepts of God, State, and Social Order.

The universality of these concepts when joined in their proper relationship is revealed not only in their projection throughout time and space, but also in the fact that the conservative groups in each country are not class parties, united by senseless economic interests. Rather, they are groups that embrace, as a synthesis of the entire nation, members of all the social strata, united by a common longing for the public welfare.

By way of explanation, let us expand upon the concepts we have listed.

God. Conservatism, which is essentially a spiritual movement, proclaims above all its faith in God, the Church, and religion, which are the immovable bases upon which social life should be founded.

The State. The state must recognize the Supreme Being as the ultimate foundation of its organization, of its laws, of its government. Only where Supreme Truth, Supreme Justice, and the Supreme Being prevail, as informing principles of the institutional system, is there true respect for the moral order, natural law, and human dignity.

Social Order. It must not be forgotten that the Church's social doctrine, repeatedly expounded in the encyclicals and papal allocutions, claims the corporative organization of economic life to be the only solution to the class struggles and injustices provoked by the capitalist system. In twenty-five years (1931-1956) the Roman pontiffs have affirmed and reaffirmed *fourteen times* that the corporative organization of professions is one of the basic points of Catholic doctrine [this controversial contention was made prior to the publication in 1961 of the recent papal social encyclical, *Mater et Magistra*]. Well then, it is evident that the natural culmination of this economic-social system is found in the homogeneous structuring of the state's political bodies, as has been realized in Spain and Portugal.

Only an authoritarian, honest, impersonal, and efficient regime, which does not represent the majority but rather the best, can instill in the masses a sense of obedience and implant in the social life the principles of order, hierarchy, and discipline, which are indispensable for attaining the common good and national progress.

Catholic Social Justice, Democracy, and Pluralism

Many Catholic leaders feel that Christian social justice can be attained only within the framework of a democracy in which the majority rules. They call for the admission of all classes into society on the basis of an equality of opportunity that is not obstructed by vote-weighting devices. They favor a structure in which there is vast social mobility, and they maintain that a greater degree of material security than traditional leaders have been willing to provide is a prerequisite for human dignity among today's masses. This has been the message of Christian Democracy in Chile, one that is supported by some and opposed by other members of that country's episcopacy. In the following selection Christian Democratic Senator Eduardo Frei disagrees with Jorge Iván Hübner as to what constitutes the Christian, moral, social system. At the same time he argues that only Christianity can provide the basis adequate to stimulate the majority of Chileans to work for the common good. This implication is resented by Chile's largest single political party, the Radical Party, which is professedly anticlerical, freethinking, and secularistic in orientation. The conservative Catholic social philosophy as advanced by Hübner, and the liberal approach as expounded by Frei, have contributed upon occasion

From Eduardo Frei Montalva, *Pensamiento y acción* (Santiago de Chile, 1958), excerpts from pp. 50-53, 70-71, and *La verdad tiene su hora* (Santiago de Chile, 4th edition, 1955), excerpts from pp. 55-66. By permission of the Editorial del Pacífico, S.A., Santiago de Chile.

to political tension, for both are critical of existing socio-politico-economic patterns.

CHRISTIANS are not newcomers to history. For two thousand years they have participated in human development. They have worked to propagate the truths contained in the Gospels, many of which are now incorporated into the social and political structures of various nations. They have, then, the temptation to defend the present order, in part created by them. Being human beings as well as Christians, it is understandable that they should try to preserve a structure which has been fashioned to some degree through their efforts. When the flesh, which is weak, commands the spirit, which sometimes abandons its role of guidance, interest in preserving and adhering to the past takes precedence over the true message of the Gospels, which is to go forward.

Thus has it been in each great period of history. At the inception of the Christian era, the followers of the new faith fought and suffered; they built their churches and monasteries, their schools and hospitals; they separated the wheat from the chaff; they brought moderation to cruel and violent men, and they transformed morality into law, law into customs, slaves into free men and self-respecting artisans, and barbarians into citizens of republics. With the passing of time, however, their energetic impulses gave way to sterile formulas; the columns supporting pristine truth were encrusted with a veneer of masonry; and words that were once used to free men were used to oppress them. In order to be able to start again, man corrupts and exhausts all that he touches, in a process like the death and rebirth of the days and the seasons. It is the tragedy of the Christian that he is present in the origin and in the final corruption of epochs.

The Christian fears the future because he knows how easy it is to destroy and how bitter and difficult it is to start again in the never-ending task of bringing about the Christian society. For this reason he turns his face nostalgically toward those models which at one time or another during the past two thousand years have succumbed to a rain of fire.

On the other hand, what have the parvenus to lose? They regard a revolution that destroys everything as an unmitigated good. Seeing only the errors and injustices of the old regime, ignorant of the dedicated and constructive efforts that certain of its leaders have taken toward directing society toward a higher level of achievement, they think only of sweeping away all that has ever been created. But it should be the dying who bury their dead and who then initiate the process of starting anew.

The creative process has always been followed by a moribund period. When the artisan guilds came into being they were, so far as was possible within the circumstances of their period, the expression of the desire for the common good and for a community of labor; they contributed toward just prices and salaries, toward stable municipal organization and high quality of production. Later, the guilds became mere skeletons that survived from the dead past, acting as obstacles to the free development of an expanding economy. Then, there came the monarchs who, in union with free men and in opposition to feudalism, fashioned the structures of European nation-states on a semi-popular basis. They did not understand that having been corrupted by the passing years, they began to oppress and to seek privilege rather than to render service. They and their partisans professed to believe that the Christian ideals, the Church, and all established values could not exist within the republican form of government, that could just be detected over the horizon in the precursory rumblings of the French revolution. At each of these turning points, it was necessary to sever the ties with the past, and to be faithful to the message to go forward. But this rupture is never easy.

During the periods of transition there are always some who look back and others who focus their gaze upon the new horizon; there are those who commit themselves to the values of the past, which within the newly emerging politico-social complex have become distorted, and those who dedicate themselves to creative activity. The task of the latter is arduous. It must be carried out with detachment; it requires the rediscovery and the interpretation of new realities. It is a part of the never-ending process which demands that the living image of permanent truth remain undistorted amidst new realities and forces.

In our own era we are witnessing this bruising process. A new historical age is being born, new forces, new facts, new men are emerging. In the era toward which the world is evolving, the over-all economy is changing its orientation. The prodigious fecundity of capitalism, nourished by Calvinism, is depleted. The state has undergone a tremendous transformation and growth, organizing and controlling the complex economic mechanism to a degree previously unknown. Change is at hand. Its universality and degree of intensity are without parallel. All of the countries of the world are in a state of agitation. In the light of this situation, it is vain to hope that the whole world will remain unaltered.

Are we going to tremble just because the world is trembling? Shall we become a statue of salt, which when it crumbles, crumbles totally? Or shall we reject the old norms of social relations, as withered leaves upon dying trees, and assimilate ourselves into the vast masses, thus reviving in society the old and always new Faith, lighted by charity, supported by the mystery of hope?

In the endeavor to change along these last-mentioned lines, within the framework of Christianity, France holds a position of singular honor. In the contemporary spiritual movement for the renovation of values and of the social influence of Christianity, France has indeed played a prominent role. Within this movement of renovation, Jacques Maritain has held the central position.

There are people in our time who never tire of speaking about democracy. Using this term, in a hackneyed sense, in all of their speeches, they have worn it out. Is democracy, government of the people, by the people, and for the people, as the great backwoodsman once described it, a living value today?

On these cold winter nights, when the water flows through the streets, I have thought about the hundreds of thousands of men, women, and children who in the mud and dampness of miserable slums and villages can barely defend the crowded hovels they live in against the freezing wind. Would they be able to believe in democracy? Would it have any significance for them? And is this the situation we are defending when we plead our devotion to democracy? Those who defend this present situation, so full of imperfections, as representing an already achieved democratic way of life are, in fact, assassinating democracy.

As the last ripple of waves that have already subsided in other continents, there has begun to circulate in our countries the belief that it is necessary to repudiate democracy, and to substitute dictatorship for it. This belief is not plainly expressed by those who espouse it, but it is implicit in their words.

Maritain has said in one of his most profound observations: "Only democracy can afford us a moral rationalization of political life, for democracy means the national organization of liberties based on law. Democracies carry with them, in a fragile bark, our earthly hope; also, I would say, the biological hope of humanity."

Here, indeed, is a fragile bark. But in it we find the only human endeavor to construct society upon the free consent and agreement of free men.

The way is difficult. Associated with democracy we can now discover unjust economic systems, horror, misery, hatred, selfishness, and overweaning ambition. The reason for this is that human society requires Christianity to a degree that it does not now possess. But simply because democracy now abounds in imperfections are we going to renounce it and abandon all hope? To place ourselves under the authority of a master would be to abandon hope.

Democracy will not be saved by those who, praising it as it now exists, petrify its abuses. Much less will it be saved by those who see only its defects and not its infinite possibilities.

Our task is to realize the possibilities of democracy, to enrich it in order to defend it. We will serve it insofar as we make it dynamic and perfect the means for the representation of all the people. We will defend it by using the goods of the nation for the advantage of all Chileans. Then, the man trembling in the night will be replaced by a citizen who can feel a sense of participation in the community and who can understand that he is part of a great family.

As it is, in each Chilean electoral campaign the politicos promise to solve, among others, the housing problem. The more they talk the worse the situation becomes, so that by now we need half a million houses to free the people from their abject misery. The only sensible thing would be to say that Chile depends on a given amount of resources of lumber, cement, steel, and labor, and to plan on this basis the actual possibilities of obtaining a definite goal within our capacity. But to establish a concrete goal implies thinking, calculating, and an effort to build the houses!

Always, the important thing seems to be to talk about what is going to be done: various reforms, immediate land distribution, instantaneous betterment. But no revolution is easy, and no serious change begins with distribution. It begins with sacrifice. As the foundation of any human creation or of any social change there must be the purifying process of sacrifice, the effort to gather the necessary material for the new building that will go up. No great good has ever come from short-term efforts to satisfy ambitions.

Really, the politicos have tried to encourage the people to consume what we didn't have, instead of encouraging them to begin by creating it. This has applied not only to material goods, but to goods of a more exalted order. In addition to creating goods capable of lightening human misery, it is necessary to train human beings to apply new techniques, to stimulate the creation of ideas capable of maintaining progressive action. Above all, it is necessary to create the moral attitude that must underlie and sustain any effort.

The "progress" based on distribution, and on spending before creating new sources of production and of vital human energies, tends to destroy one system of labor without substituting another for it. At most, it transfers activities from the private onto the public level. This results in a hybrid system in which no one knows the limits of the "collective" and of the "individual," and in which the incentives that motivated capitalism are not replaced by the incentives of a totalitarian regime. And so a society is created in which the authority, lacking purpose and goals, is always in transition and trying only to sustain itself a bit longer. Only the concept of the common good can give lasting authority to government. Without this, the interest groups come to dictate the manner in which authority is exercised.

In this way society slowly falls apart, for lack of the cement of common interest. Feudal forces, economic interest groups, and labor union power-blocs appear and begin to fatten. We retrogress to a system of divided communities, as in the first stages of medieval times, when the concept of the nation was still unknown. To have a nation we need more than the physical fact of territory with its boundaries and a given number of people to populate it. We need also a common interest so that the people will perform a collective labor motivated by the same reasons.

The requisite condition for the existence of a nation is missing when the unchecked egotism of privileged groups is the dominant power in society. Under these circumstances, the feeling of solidarity is absent, and the proletariat can never even approach the fringe of those benefits enjoyed by upper and middle classes. It is not surprising, therefore, that even though the political constitution of the state guarantees the equality of all before the law, the laws establish more favorable provisions for those who earn more and live better than for those who earn less and live worse. This curious paradox, viewed in indifference by almost everyone, explains how a nation can cease to be an organic whole.

In Chile, the worker who has the shortest life expectancy must reach the age of sixty-five to obtain an extremely small pension, while in the groups of longest life expectancy one may retire before age fifty with a handsome income lasting the rest of his life. Chile is already in the stage in which national disintegration is fully evident.

If we examine reality we see that there are no common motives that move all the sectors of the people. We can almost affirm the contrary. It is enough for one social group to favor an idea to evoke suspiciousness, if not open antagonism toward it, among the other groups.

If our country lacks common motives, it also lacks leaders who know how to lead and who have the moral integrity that is necessary to command respect and to impose constructive norms. We lack the spiritual hierarchy of values which must underlie effort that is genuinely conducive toward the common good. Inevitably, the result is collective disorganization, and the disappearance of criteria by which to determine what is convenient for the people. Thus, authority becomes so weak that every day in order to survive it must keep every petitioner happy, paying no attention to any over-all, guiding principle of national well-being.

These petty transactions, naturally, cannot please everyone. And so discontent becomes a permanent state of the collective spirit. There comes a moment in which no activity is carried out with efficiency. All of the functional interest groups are pervaded by an attitude of constant complaint, rather than animated toward action by optimistic expectations.

If we go through the cities of the country we shall see that all of them need water, schools, jails, public services, roads, and the like. The politicos promise all these things to them simultaneously, despite the abundance of evidence that material resources and trained personnel are inadequate to solve these problems even one at a time.

Nobody should be so naïve as to believe that all these difficulties could be overcome simultaneously. But the evidence shows that there does not exist so much as a progressive, step-by-step, logical plan designed to facilitate the future solution of these numerous problems. The government functionary, the worker, the businessman, all know that they could do far more. But they continue to produce the minimum, embittered by the prevailing uncertainty and by the seeming permanence of a plethora of vexing difficulties that need not exist.

In summary, we do no feel the presence of the kingdom of justice among ourselves. Everyone has the sensation that the country is not going as it should and that he is not offered the necessary opportunities. The malaise does not affect exclusively the economic situation, but also the spirit of every man and woman. Sufficient evidence of this is the fact that even many of those who live in prosperity are discontent.

It is true that we have in Chile an atmosphere of excessive criticism. It is also true that the human heart will never be satisfied. But there must be a proportion in all things, and one may venture to say that in Chile discontent has grown out of all proportion. A contemptuous, cynical form of criticism creeps forward among our people. A country cannot live on consoling promises. And it offers very little hope to people to tell them that they live in a democracy, when it is a frightened, demoralized democracy.

Some try to reassure themselves by rationalizing that, after all, we have always been this way, and we cannot really fight, for example, chronic inflation. But the concrete fact is that we find ourselves without roads, houses, and water for our towns. All these problems are the accumulated fruit of this rationalization, and of the prevailing ignorance and overwhelming misery of a vast section of the people.

That is why it is not enough to talk about our democratic regime. We cannot live indefinitely on words. Our attempt to do so is precisely why every day the gulf between the two social groups in our country grows wider and wider.

There is no doubt that a great deal of what is happening in Latin America is implied in the process described by Arnold Toynbee, who maintains that one factor involved in the collapse of a civilization is the presence in it of an internal proletariat, a group that is in society but not of society. Certainly there is a proletariat within our societies that is not a part of them. This is noticeable throughout our lands. Whoever has experienced life in the Latin American countries can readily observe at every moment the horizontal divide that separates those who belong to society from those who are aliens. At any moment of our national existence we can show that the reactions of this alienated proletariat are quite different from those of the men who rule the community. This proletariat is completely foreign to, completely beyond the sphere of influence of the ideas and feelings that move the community.

In order to acquire and preserve the precious gifts of freedom and democracy it is necessary to incorporate this proletariat into the national existence, to make it a part of the whole people. Only by living in integral unity can people defend freedom and democracy. Otherwise, their lives will become every day more miserable. The barbarians are never far distant from decadent societies, and they will not be deterred by the flimsy defensive walls erected against them.

Social Justice and
Christian Democracy in México

Certain Catholic leaders in Mexico, clergymen and laymen, are turning increasingly to the idea that Christian social justice, as formulated and explained by the Catholic Church, is the only adequate means of stemming communism. Their criticism of the incumbent, official political party (Partido Revolucionario Institucional) for having failed to concern itself adequately and intelligently with social justice is angering PRI politicians, and certain extremists are beginning to mutter that the time has come once again to start putting priests in jail. Thus, old tensions are being revived. The main opposition party in Mexico is the Church-oriented Party of National Action (Partido de Acción Nacional), or the PAN. In the following selection from a publication of its youth organization, Mexicans are exhorted to return to their national culture and traditions. This is actually a call to restore the influence of Catholicism. The voice of political opposition in Mexico is assuming distinctly religious overtones.

IT has been accepted as a foregone conclusion that poverty and oppression are fertile grounds for the spread of communist propaganda. It is therefore necessary to observe, by examining some points of principal

From Organización Juvenil del Partido de Acción Nacional, *La penetración comunista en México* (México, D.F., 1960), excerpts from pp. 1-25 of the pamphlet. By permission of the Organización Juvenil del Partido de Acción Nacional.

importance, what the true status of the Mexican people is.

The gross national income for 1960 is estimated at approximately 120 billion pesos, which if divided equally among the some 35,000,000 inhabitants of the republic would constitute an individual income for the year of 3,450 pesos, or $276. By way of comparison, the annual average individual income in the United States is approximately $2,990. It is readily apparent that our individual income is about one-tenth of what it is in the United States. In Mexico the situation is further aggravated by the uneven distribution of wealth.

According to data obtained from the 1950 census (1960 figures have not yet been made public), the national income was distributed as follows: 1.5 percent of the population had a monthly income of more than $120; 3.5 percent had a monthly income of between $64 and $120; 12 percent earned a monthly income of between $32 and $64. On the other hand, 83 percent of the people earned between $6 and $32 a month.

Far from being corrected in the past ten years, the unjust distribution of wealth has assumed more striking proportions, because salaries have not kept pace with inflation. If we take 100 as our base number, the cost of food between 1939 and 1957 went up from 100 to 616.3, and clothing went up to 642.4. Meantime, the average salary increased only to 469. This is a clear indication that real salaries have decreased. This condition has further increased the disproportion between that small sector which accumulates great profits and that which is made up of the bulk of the population.

The following data, taken only by way of example, afford an idea of the privations which Mexicans must endure. According to a study published by Eduardo Huarte, *Renta y alimentación de la familia rural en México* ["The Income and Nutrition of the Rural Family in Mexico"], a typical family composed of five persons requires a daily diet of some 12,430 calories in order to be properly fed. Given current food prices, this means that the family would have to spend $1.56 a day on food in order to have an adequate diet. It so happens that the minimum salary for the rural region surrounding Mexico City is only $1.14 per day; and there are certain regions to the South in which the daily minimum salary is only $0.40.

We cite the following shocking case as an example of rural conditions. Farmers in the state of Hidalgo which has the advantage of financial backing furnished by the National Bank of Ejidal Credit were able to gain an average family income of only $14.88 during the year of 1958. These figures are based on records kept by this bank.

As to general housing needs, it will suffice to mention that only 17 percent of the housing in Mexico is considered to be of adequate construction. Furthermore, only 17 percent of residential construction in the country is serviced by water and sewage systems. The rise in population requires an increase of some 200,000 new dwellings per year. This, of course, is far more than we can at present provide.

A certain sign of the miserable living conditions now prevailing in the country is the fact that several hundred thousand farm laborers (*braceros*) will migrate to the United States to work there. Nor is there any way of telling how many additional thousands would leave this country if they could obtain the required contract.

Unfortunately, the cultural situation is no better than the material conditions described above. United Nations studies made in Mexico during 1959 show that we had in this country approximately 8,635,000 children of grade-school age (between the ages of five and fourteen). To educate the number of children in this group who were in the position of being able to attend school, at least 5,181,000 grade-school openings would have been necessary. It so happened that only 4,436,-000 children were able to register that year. By adding to these figures the truancy factor, it is possible to begin to arrive at some comprehension of the magnitude of this problem. According to figures released by the Official Eleven-Year Plan Commission, of those children enrolled in the first grade, only 49.6 percent pass on to the second grade, and only 13.5 percent reach the sixth grade, while only one in a thousand will ever receive a degree.

The situation of post-primary education is even worse. There are approximately 6,366,000 young men and women between the ages of fifteen and twenty-four, with only 255,000 school openings for them. In the United States, 86.9 percent of the youth in the appropriate age group attend high school, while in Mexico only 8.1 percent can do so.

According to information furnished by the National Teacher's Capability Institute, only 32 percent of those people now teaching in Mexico have a degree [from high school]. It would be necessary to train about 6,300 teachers annually to care adequately for our growing needs. At present we have facilities to train only 3,100 per year.

A direct consequence of this situation is the large increase in juvenile delinquency. Contributing also to this is poverty and the materialistic tone of instruction imparted through the years to our youth in the public schools.

The political situation in Mexico is as bad as or worse than the material and cultural conditions. However, it cannot be revealed by statistics. It is necessary, therefore, to point out certain unquestionable facts which will enable the reader to gain some comprehension of the vast political suppression that now prevails in Mexico.

Article 3 of the Mexican constitution prevents the head of a family from educating his children according to his convictions or beliefs. Section 2 of this Article prohibits the teaching of grade, high-school, or university curricula to farm or laboring classes without the special authorization of the state. This authorization can be denied or revoked without recourse to appeal. According to Section 4 of this same Article, "religious corporations, ministers . . . , or those societies allied with teaching or propagating some creed or religion, may not in any way participate in those primary or high schools or trade schools engaged in educating the farm or laboring classes."

Article 5 of the Mexican constitution prohibits "the establishment of monastic orders, regardless of creed or reason for creating them."

Article 6 proclaims the freedom of thought and expression, asserting that no judicial or administrative sanctions will limit this freedom. Nevertheless, secondary laws expressly prohibit religious expression outside the temple and at the same time drastically curtail activities of a religious character.

The right of assembly, guaranteed by Article 9 of the constitution, is nullified in practice by police rulings that prohibit the calling of meetings without special permission from the authorities.

The Church in Mexico has no private rights. It has no legal personality and therefore cannot appeal to any courts of justice or enter into any private contracts. Articles 27 and 130 are an affront to any church or religion.

It is at once apparent that this situation is not in keeping, either in fact or in practice, with the Universal Declaration of the Rights of Man, to which Mexico as a member of the United Nations has publicly subscribed.

Mexico has never been able to enjoy the fruitful benefits of democracy, or even of a law-abiding government. On the contrary, open or disguised dictators, tyrants and the like, have always been, and are still, in full control of the government. These men manage to remain in power by the force of police-state methods and, upon occasion, because of the apathy and bungling methods of the United States which contribute to the support of these dictators.

These social, economic, and political conditions go begging for justice in our country, and in the absence of a satisfactory solution seek an answer in the never-never land of the communist world.

Ever since its inception, and particularly in these critical times, the Party of National Action (PAN) has proclaimed that the only genuine and effective way to curb the spread of communism in Mexico is to make a valiant and consistent effort to provide social justice based on integrity and honesty of purpose. The goals of the PAN are to provide, among other points, a decent minimum wage for labor and rural workers; the participation of labor in the profits of the employer, as well as all of the other benefits provided within a Christian Democratic structure. Our party wishes to establish a sound and stable basis of operation for the worker and the investor in order to raise the standard of living of our people and to bring about a more equitable distribution of our national wealth.

Truly significant problems, such as housing, education, and in general all of those difficulties arising from our rapid increase in population, cannot be resolved by the state, regardless of its centralization of efforts and the proliferation of official programs. It is necessary to do away with all legal stumbling blocks which prevent or limit the participation of the people themselves in working to solve these problems. Only in this way will it be possible to establish the requisite conditions for enjoyment of the rights to life, liberty, and pursuit of happiness.

There is only one effective and proper way to destroy communism, and that is to respect the will of the people and to guarantee the free expression of the different political parties.

In conclusion, the Youth Organization of the PAN:*

1. Denounces before national and world opinion the grave and imminent danger that communism will take over the destinies of the Mexican people.

2. Denounces and condemns the government's in-

---

* Seven points were included in the pamphlet, four of which are reduced below. [Editor's note.]

difference to the national problems and its efforts to stamp out the legitimate freedoms of the people. All of this contributes to the advantage of the communist movement. We protest also against the political tendency to exalt the state, and the lack of a true ideology and consistent planning within the administration.

3. Calls upon all forces and sections of our country to unite in a solid front to fight for the national culture and traditions.

4. Finally, in the face of the communist menace, the Youth Organization of the PAN proclaims that the only way in which social justice can be attained at the same time liberty is preserved is through Christian Democracy.

ROBERT E. SCOTT

Social Justice Without
Christian Democracy in Mexico

A political scientist at the University of Illinois, Robert E. Scott has conducted extensive research in Mexico and other Latin American countries. He feels that the Mexican revolutionary movement that began in 1910 has accomplished much that is positive and beneficial. Only since the Revolution, he contends, has Mexico developed a truly national ideology, one capable of uniting different sectors in the effort to work toward national well-being. The political background of the PAN, as described by Scott, has been of such a nature as to raise doubts among many Mexicans as to the sincerity of the party in its rather recently assumed interest in social justice and democracy. Scott also shows that there is no unanimous voice of Church-oriented political opposition in Mexico. One traditional proclerical party, the Nationalist Party, has accommodated itself to the existing situation, and has been able to work advantageously within it.

THE intellectual spokesmen of the [Mexican] Revolution range from one end of the political spectrum to the other, each vocally defending his own discrete interpretation of the movement. Some, such as Rafael Nieto and Luis Cabrera, were among the radical majority in the constitutional convention at Querétero

From Robert E. Scott, *Mexican Government in Transition* (Urbana, Illinois, 1959), excerpts from pp. 99-101, 110-111, 182-187. By permission of the University of Illinois Press.

during 1917; others, such as Graciano Sánchez and Vicente Lombardo Toledano, represent left-radical agrarian and labor emphasis in the revolution. Another group, which included such men as José Vasconcelos and Manuel Gómez Morín, began in the revolutionary camp, working with such middle-class leaders as [Gonzalo] Obregón and [Plutarco Elías] Calles, but reacted in an increasingly conservative manner to later attempts at basic social and economic change. Gómez Morín, for example, was one of the founders of the National Action Party (the PAN), which is the principal opposition party in Mexico.

During the formative years of the Revolution, in the absence of a complete revolutionary philosophy of their own, some Mexicans adopted Marxian terminology. This, together with the anticapitalist, anti-Church, and xenophobic phases of the Revolution, long made the revolutionary governments more than a little suspect in the camps of the liberal democracies. Many, probably most, of these actions and attitudes were, however, more nearly negative manifestations of a positive nationalistic fervor or the reaction of rising leaders to attempts on the part of conservative institutions to limit their power than vital factors in a consistent revolutionary program. Over the years, certainly, basic Mexican values have pushed themselves relentlessly to the fore, forcing alien concepts to give way before them.

This does not suggest that there are no Communists in Mexico. There are, just as there are *sinarquistas* [conservative Catholic elements who at one time showed fascistic leanings] and others of the extreme right. It does suggest, however, that in spite of a few vociferous extremists on both ends of the political spectrum, the Revolution set at work forces that could produce a truly Mexican nation, with its own values and institutions. More important, that nation now includes a larger proportion than ever before of Mexicans who share more or less similar values. And, almost by definition, widely shared values are moderate values, especially in politics. The Revolution has succeeded finally in producing such an ideology.

For all its contradictions, the spirit of the Revolution has caught and held the imaginations of most Mexicans. It has become one of those social myths through which hope in tomorrow's promise outweighs today's failures. Perhaps its very strength lies in the lack of any pre-fixed dogma, which has allowed revolutionary values and goals to be modified over the years to meet the needs of a people in flux.

The revolutionary governments have been far from perfect in their execution of substantive policies and even less so in their political morals. But such an evaluation must be weighed in the context of the environment in which the revolutionary system has evolved. Some of the Mexicans who find today's politics wanting are measuring the Revolution's accomplishments against very nearly impossible ideal goals, rather than against the problems of the past. Others who object to the new politics are in opposition to the Revolution as such, rather than to specific policies. Both of these groups fail to recognize the degree to which both material and political progress have affected Mexico since 1910, and the very real problems which have had to be conquered before this progress could be attained.

The revolutionary tenets and actions which are most frequently cited to demonstrate the failings of the Revolution and its leaders are indeed questionable. They must include such things as persecution of the Church, expropriation of large private land holdings to provide collective farms, government control over subsoil mineral rights, and even the expropriation of the foreign-owned petroleum operations in Mexico. But each of these actions, if considered in context, was an attempt to offset one or another counterrevolutionary influence or interest which was in itself unrepresentative of the general population or the national interest.

As the revolutionary values and the governments which represent them have consolidated their positions, the most radical applications of these acts have eased or disappeared. The beginnings of a working agreement with a less politically motivated Church, or perhaps one that no longer holds so predominant a position in the more complex society, have made their appearance.

*   *   *   *   *

The *Partido de Acción Nacional*, formed in 1939, is an outgrowth of the right-opposition movement that grew bolder and more active with the return of political stability and the increase of pressure upon vested interests as President [Lázaro] Cárdenas [1934-1940] perfected the organization of the revolutionary party. Originally, the PAN was a small but disproportionately influential organization of conservative intellectuals and professional men, banded together by Manuel Gómez Morín, who opposed the sharp turn to the left made by the revolutionary government under Cárdenas.

In entering active presidential politics [which it did not do until 1952], the PAN had both to expand its membership and to change its form of organization; in doing so it had also to broaden the nature of its appeal. *Acción Nacional* always had been known as a conservative party, representing the interests of the Church, big business, and upper- and middle-class professional people. To broaden its membership base, either existing functional interest associations had to be attracted to the PAN or new ones sponsored by it and members recruited.

During the 1952 presidential campaign, given the difficulties of organizing a widely based party in the face of a vigorously operating political machine like that of the PRI, *Acción Nacional* seemed to be quite successful. Its political alliance with the *Unión Nacional Sinarquista*, one faction of the right-wing, nationalist *sinarquista* movement that had splintered a short while previously, provided the PAN with ready-made entree into certain rural areas in return for a few nominations to congressional seats. Dissatisfaction with the leadership of some unions in the PRI's labor sector, together with pressure from their conservative bosses, led to the formation of at least token labor union support, especially in the state of Nuevo León, where Monterey's industrial ownership is strongly pro-PAN.

Once the election had been lost, however, the façade began to crumble. The multitude of problems inherent in attempting to satisfy overlapping and often conflicting demands of the expanded membership, especially without the advantage of government patronage, were beyond the ability of the loosely organized and poorly disciplined coalition. Worse still, entry into active political campaigning had driven a wedge into the unified leadership of the old, elite group that had dominated the party from its foundation. Part, headed by the 1952 presidential candidate, Efraín González Luna, harked back to *Acción Nacional*'s original concept of intransigent and permanent opposition to the revolutionary party and everything it stands for, an attitude not unlike the rigid antirevolutionary views of the *sinarquistas*. Another faction, personified in Gómez Morín, saw that possible advantages could accrue to the PAN by participating in the existing political system as a "loyal" opposition; they hoped thereby to win greater consideration for the interests they represented and a louder voice in policy-making councils, even at the cost of making peace with the Revolution.

This latter, more Westernized portion of the party won its point, but at the cost of alienating the last mass organization that had supported the PAN; the 150,000 members of the *Unión Nacional Sinarquista* were ordered to participate in the UNS campaign of political reform, but to support no presidential candidate during the 1958 election. The *sinarquistas* always had been somewhat suspicious of the "intellectuals" of the PAN, whom they feared were manipulating the less sophisticated members of their movement.

Despite the efforts of the Gómez Morín faction, therefore, of necessity in 1958 *Acción Nacional* reverted from its 1952 role as a true (if hopeless) electoral machine to that of a political gadfly. Luis H.

Alvarez waged a vociferous and driving campaign, incorporating sweeping revolutionary-style demands for land reform, labor benefits, social welfare, and other popular causes, but this time the PAN never really managed to attract any organized mass support. Keenly disappointed by the poor showing made by its congressional candidates as well as by the presidential nominee, many national leaders returned to their previous attitudes of intransigence.

At the PAN's fourteenth national convention, held in the Mexican capital during March, 1959, the split between the two factions became a struggle for control of the party. The more moderate supporters of Gómez Morín, who sought to make *Acción Nacional* a more nearly Western-style party, operating within the context of the existing political system, were defeated by a coalition of the González Luna Old Guard and most of the youth section, led by Felipe Gómez Mont. The victorious group adopted a policy of "direct action" in which the PAN declared open political warfare on the revolutionary party with the most vigorous attacks possible. This direct action took the form of irresponsible and vicious attacks upon the policies and candidates of the revolutionary party during the state and local elections held in Baja California, Chihuahua, and elsewhere.

At the same convention Lic. José González Torres was elected the party's president. González Torres, who had been Secretary General of the PAN and president of three Catholic lay organizations, the Catholic Association of Young Mexicans, *Pax Romana*, and Catholic Action, was given a broader measure of authority over the party than his predecessor had wielded, for both the National Council and the National Executive Committee's functions were reduced to primarily consultative organs.

In short, the National Action Party seems to have traveled a circular route from elite group to more popularly based movement and back to intransigent and narrow opposition, once again meriting its popular designation as *club bancario*, "the banker's club." At the same time, as the revolutionary party itself becomes more and more moderate and middle-class, it absorbs many of the smaller businessmen and industrialists who once found a political haven in the PAN. Somewhat the same is true of Mexico's Roman Catholics; long strides have been taken down the road to adjustment between Church and Revolution. If it is still rather difficult for highly orthodox Mexicans to act politically through the official party, *Acción Nacional* now must share its role as spokesman for Church interests not only with the *sinarquistas*, whose movement was refused recognition as a national political party in 1954, but with the Mexican Nationalist Party, which is legally recognized.

The *Partido Nacionalista de México* calls itself an opposition party and between elections makes noises like one, but during both 1952 and 1958 it "reluctantly" supported the official candidate, though not necessarily the platform upon which he ran.

The stated thesis of the PNM is "to unite the Mexican Revolution with Christianity," a goal which the leadership of the movement seems to have followed for the past thirty years, first outside and now, since 1950, within the official fold.

That this group, with its long history of ideas, with its support of clerical authority and its attacks upon Article 3 and other parts of the Mexican constitution designed to promote secularization of the country, with its espousal of the *hispanidad* so odious to revolutionary Mexicans because of its identification with old-style conservatism, should be able to accommodate itself within the revolutionary coalition (if not in the party itself), and that the PRI should accept it, speaks volumes for the level of political pragmatism that Mexico has achieved.

Or perhaps it is pragmatism tinged with a dose of healthy cynicism, for there are those who accuse the PNM of having sold itself to the official party for economic advantages and patronage. Certainly it is

difficult to understand how a party representing so
specialized an interest should be able to attract the
necessary membership, much less amass the funds it
spends, unless it has some unknown source of aid. And
it is advantageous for the PRI to have an ally that
helps weaken the opposition claims that the revolutionary movement is antireligious.

Whatever the motivation, the Nationalist Party has
used its semi-allied position to press upon the revolutionary party strong anti-Communist viewpoints. It
helped spark the gradual replacement of pro-Red textbooks that was begun in 1953, and continued this role
through the 1958 presidential campaign, in which its
principal theme was anti-communism. In this sense the
PNM is accomplishing its primary educational function even though its electoral influence may be mini-
mal.

Suggestions for Additional Reading

I. THE COLONIAL PERIOD

Chapter X, "The Church in America," in Clarence H. Haring, *The Spanish Empire in America* (published originally in New York in 1947 and in a new paperback edition in 1963), offers an outstanding treatment of the institutional structure of the Church as well as its relations to the state in colonial Hispanic America. Important bibliographical suggestions are also included. Chapter IV, "The Church," in William L. Schurz, *This New World* (New York, 1945), furnishes many penetrating insights. W. Eugene Shiels, S.J., *King and Church: The Rise and Fall of the Patronato Real* (Chicago, 1961), reproduces the important documents pertaining to the *patronato real*, and occasionally introduces short explanatory sections. A broader treatment of the Church in colonial Hispanic America can be found in Lucas Ayarragaray, *La iglesia en América y la dominación española* (Buenos Aires, 1935), and the American Academy of Franciscan History, *Studies Presented at the Conference on the History of Religion in the New World during Colonial Times* (Washington, D.C., 1958). France V. Scholes, *Church and State in New Mexico, 1610-1670*, 2 vols. (Albuquerque, N.M., 1937-1945), records examples of bitter conflict between the two powers. Comparable material is found in J. H. Parry, *The Audiencia in Nueva Galicia in the Sixteenth Century: A Study in Spanish Colonial Government* (Cambridge, Eng., 1948). Chapter XIV, "The Cabildo and the Church," in J. Preston Moore, *The Cabildo in Peru under the Hapsburgs, 1530-1700* (Durham, N.C., 1954), describes the frequent friction between Church and municipal officials, while Frederick B. Pike, "Public Work and Social Welfare in Colonial Spanish American Towns," *The Americas*, XII (April, 1957), contends that Church-state relations at this level were often cordial.

Useful articles dealing with Church-state relations in colonial Hispanic America include: Julius Klein, "The Church in Spanish American History," *Catholic Historical Review*, III (October, 1917); J. Lloyd Mecham, "The Colonial Church," in A. C. Wilgus, editor, *Colonial Hispanic America* (Washington, D.C., 1936); Robert Charles Padden, "The Ordenanza del Patronazgo,

1574: an Interpretative Essay," *The Americas,* XII (April, 1956). Particularly valuable for revealing the tension that existed between peninsular and creole churchmen within the various religious orders is Antonine Tibesar, O.F.M., "The *Alternativa*: A Study in Spanish-Creole Relations in Seventeenth-Century Peru," *The Americas,* XI (January, 1955).

An excellent account of Church-state relations in Brazil from colonial times to 1890 is in J. Dornas Filho, *O padroado e a igreja brasileira* (São Paulo, 1939). This subject receives attention also in M. Cardozo, "The Dependency, 1500-1808," Lawrence H. Hill, editor, *Brazil* (Berkeley, Calif., 1947), H. V. Livermore, "The Portuguese Expansion in the New World," Vol. I, *Cambridge Modern History* (London, 1957), and Charles Wagley, "The Indian Heritage of Brazil," in T. Lynn Smith and Alexander Marchant, editors, *Brazil, Portrait of Half a Continent* (New York, 1951). The history of the Jesuits in Brazil, 1549-1762, is painstakingly narrated by Serafim Leite, *Historia da Companhia de Jesus no Brasil,* 10 vols. (Lisbon and Rio de Janeiro, 1938-1960).

For material on the Inquisition in Ibero America, consult what is probably the most important work of José Toribio Medina on the subject, *Historia del Tribunal de la Inquisición de Lima, 1569-1820,* 2 vols. (Santiago de Chile, 1956 edition). Alfonso Junco, *Inquisición sobre la inquisición* (México, D.F., 1949), examines the writings of historians who have attacked and defended the Inquisition, and is somewhat sympathetic to the institution. Outspokenly critical of it is Boleslao Lewin, *El Santo Oficio en América y el más grande proceso inquisitorial en el Perú* (Buenos Aires, 1950). In Chapter VII of *Baroque Times in Old Mexico* (Ann Arbor, Mich., 1959), Irving A. Leonard describes some of the police-court activities of the Inquisition. Richard E. Greenleaf, *Zumárraga and the Mexican Inquisition* (Washington, D.C., 1961), is an enlightening work on the early operations of the Inquisition in Mexico, before the Holy Office Tribunal was officially established in 1569. Cecil Roth, *History of the Marranos* (Philadelphia, 1941), and Arnold Wiznitzer, *Jews in Colonial Brazil* (New York, 1960), relate the activities of the Inquisition in Brazil against those suspected of practicing the Jewish faith.

Catholic missionary work in Ibero America frequently led to clashes with state functionaries, and also to controversy among the different religious orders. Moreover, writers have long disagreed over the ultimate effects of missionary activity upon the aboriginal population. One of the best essays describing the broader aspects of missionary activity is Herbert E. Bolton, "The Mission as a Frontier Institution in the Spanish American Colonies," in Bolton, *Wider Horizons of American History* (New York, 1939). Magnus Mörner, *The Political and Economic Activities of the Jesuits in the La Plata Region: the Hapsburg Era,* translated by Albert Read (Stockholm, 1953), John Leddy Phelan, *The Millennial Kingdom of the Franciscans in the New World* (Berkeley, Calif., 1956), and Mathias C. Kiemen, O.F.M., *The Indian Policy of Portugal in the Amazon Region, 1614-1693* (Washington, D.C., 1954), touch upon the conflicts that frequently accompanied missionary endeavor. J. Fred Rippy and Jean Thomas Nelson, *Crusaders of the Jungle* (Chapel Hill, N.C., 1936), Charles S. Braden, *Religious Aspects of the Conquest of Mexico* (Durham, N.C., 1930), and Robert Ricard, *La conquista espiritual de México,* translated from French by Ángel María Garibay (Mexico, D.F., 1947), describe early missionary activity in favorable terms. Richard N. Adams, "Freedom and Reform in Rural Latin America," in F. B. Pike, editor, *Freedom and Reform in Latin America* (Notre Dame, Ind., 1959), and John Howland Rowe, "The Incas under Spanish Colonial Institutions," *Hispanic American Historical Review,* XXXVII (May, 1957) suggest that the over-all effects of colonial Church activity among the Indians was largely negative. Frequently, the endeavors of churchmen to protect the aborigines in areas already conquered and settled led to clashes with civil authorities. For some examples of this see Lewis Hanke, *The Spanish Struggle for Justice in the Conquest of America* (Philadelphia, 1959).

Conflict of opinion over the role played by the Church in the Spanish Indies arises from the manner in which writers judge the general character of the colonial system. Those who are critical of this colonial venture are generally hostile to the Church. In this category should be included Felipe Barreda Laos, *Vida intelectual del virreinato del Perú* (Buenos Aires, 1937); Rufino Blanco-Fombona, *El conquistador español del siglo XVI: ensayo de interpretación* (Madrid, 1922), and Genaro García, *Carácter de la conquista española en América y en México, según los textos de los historiadores primitivos* (Mexico, D.F., 1901). Works that emphasize the positive contributions of Iberian colonization and praise the role of the Church include: Constantino Bayle, S.J., *España en América* (Madrid, 1942); Rómulo D. Carbia, *Historia eclesiástica del Rio de la Plata,* 2 vols. (Buenos Aires, 1935), and *Historia de la leyenda negra hispano-americana* (Buenos Aires, 1943); Guillermo Furlong Cardiff, S.J., *Nacimiento y desarrollo de la filosofía en el Rio de la Plata, 1536-1810* (Buenos Aires, 1952); Julio Tobar Donoso, *La iglesia, modeladora de la nacionalidad* (Quito, Ecuador, 1953).

II. THE FIRST CENTURY
OF INDEPENDENCE AND
III. THE CONTEMPORARY SCENE

The book with which to begin the study of Church-state relations in the national period is J. Lloyd Mecham, *Church and*

State in Latin America (Chapel Hill, N.C., 1934). The first chapter of the work is devoted to the colonial period, and the second and third to the role of the Church in the independence movement. The remainder of the book deals entirely with the national period. Considerably less comprehensive and scholarly is E. Ryan, *The Church in the South American Republics* (Milwaukee, 1932). On the role of the Church in the period of the wars of independence, see Mecham, "The Papacy and Spanish American Independence," *Hispanic American Historical Review*, IX (May, 1929), and Karl M. Schmitt, "The Clergy and the Independence of New Spain," *ibid.*, XXXIV (1954). See also Pedro Leturia, *El ocaso del patronato real en la América española* (Madrid, 1925). For a rather extreme example of the conservative viewpoint, as expressed from the dawn of independence, that the Church must virtually dominate the state, see J. Fernández de Landa, *Las relaciones entre la iglesia y el estado* (Buenos Aires, 1958).

The Mexican Church-state controversy has produced more polemical than sound historical writing. An outspoken apology for the Church is Mariano Cuevas, S.J., *Historia de la iglesia en México*, 5 vols. (El Paso, Tex., 1928), which carries the story from colonial times to 1910. A passionate denunciation of the Mexican Church and clergy is found in Alfonso Toro, *La iglesia y el estado en México: estudio sobre los conflictos entre el clero católico y los gobiernos mexicanos desde la independencia hasta nuestros días* (Mexico, D.F., 1927). Scholarly treatment of the topic can be found in W. H. Callcott, *Church and State in Mexico, 1822-1857* (Durham, N.C., 1926), and *Liberalism in Mexico, 1857-1929* (Stanford, Calif., 1931); Earl K. James, "Church and State in Mexico," *The Annals of the American Academy of Political and Social Science*, Vol. 208 (March, 1940); Sister Elizabeth Ann Rice, *The Diplomatic Relations between the United States and Mexico, as Affected by the Struggle for Religious Liberty in Mexico, 1925-1929* (Washington, D.C., 1959); Robert E. Quirk, *The Mexican Revolution and the Catholic Church, 1910-1929* (Bloomington, forthcoming); Karl M. Schmitt, "Catholic Adjustment to the Secular State," *Catholic Historical Review*, XLVII (July, 1962); Walter V. Scholes, *Mexican Politics during the Juárez Regime* (Columbia, Mo., 1957). Partisan feelings have crept into textbooks by United States authors. H. B. Parkes, *A History of Mexico* (Boston, 1938, and later editions) occasionally shows anticlerical bias, while H. L. Schlarman (the late bishop of Peoria, Illinois), *Mexico, the Land of Volcanoes* (Milwaukee, 1951), abandons historical objectivity in defending the Church and clergymen. Various Mexican works pertaining to the Church-state question are discussed in the excellent article by Robert Potash, "The Historiography of Mexico since 1821," *Hispanic American Historical Review*, XI (August, 1960).

Colombia was another country plagued by a protracted and bitter Church-state controversy. One aspect of this story is related by Carey Shaw, Jr., "Church and State in Colombia ∿s Observed by American Diplomats, 1834-1906," *Hispanic American Historical Review*, XXI, No. 4 (November, 1941), 577-613. Strongly defending the clergymen are José Manuel Groot, *Historia eclesiástica y civil de Nueva Granada*, 5 vols. (Bogota, 1953 3d.), dealing with the colonial period and the national period up to 1830, and J. Iván Cadavid G., *Los fueros de la iglesia ante el liberalismo y el conservatismo en Colombia: evolución político-religiosa de nuestros dos partidos, 1837-1955* (Medellín, 1955). The anticlerical viewpoint is expressed in Jorge Ospina Londoño, *Pascual Bravo: los partidos políticos en Colombia* (Medellín, 1938). Ecuador's most controversial figure in Church-state relations is Gabriel García Moreno, who in the second half of the nineteenth century bestowed upon the Church a more exalted position than it had enjoyed in colonial times. Favorable works dealing with García Moreno are J. J. Horgan, *Great Catholic Laymen* (New York, 1905), Richard Pattee, *Gabriel García Moreno y el Ecuador de su tiempo* (Quito, 1941), and Julio Tobar Donoso, *La iglesia ecuatoriana en el siglo XIX* (Quito, 1934). Perhaps even more bitterly critical of García Moreno than the celebrated Juan Montalvo, the nineteenth-century Ecuadoran intellectual who forcefully denounced the tyranny which allegedly gripped Ecuador, 1860-1875, is Benjamín Carrión, *García Moreno, el santo del patíbulo* (Mexico, D.F., Buenos Aires, 1959). A general survey that is friendly to the Church is Juan Ignacio Larrea, *La iglesia y el estado en el Ecuador* (Sevilla, 1954). Church and state have quarreled frequently in Venezuela, and this story is told authoritatively in Mary Watters, *A History of the Church in Venezuela, 1810-1930* (Chapel Hill, N.C., 1933).

John J. Kennedy, *Catholicism, Nationalism and Democracy in Argentina* (Notre Dame, Ind., 1958), analyzes currents of Catholic political philosophy in Argentina, asserts that many churchmen there have favored democracy, and reports skillfully on the Perón vs. the Church issue. A valuable study that frequently touches on Church-state relations in the early national period is Joseph T. Criscenti, *Argentine Constitutional History, 1810-1852* (Boston, 1961). José S. Campobassi, *Laicismo y catolicismo en la educación pública argentina* (Buenos Aires, 1961), deals with the growth of religious freedom and secular education, 1810-1885. The clergy was divided on these issues. A surprising number of churchmen favored religious freedom and secular education, probably as a means of encouraging immigration and bringing about rapid national development. Arthur P. Whitaker, *Argentine Upheaval: Perón's Fall and the New Régime* (New York, 1956), carefully describes the clash between Perón and the Church. Some of the literature published in

Argentina that deals with this topic is discussed in Fritz Hoff-man, "Perón and After," *Hispanic American Historical Review*, XXXVI (November, 1956). A discussion of earlier published works in Argentina, Paraguay and Uruguay, many of which refer to the Church-state issue, is Joseph R. Barager, "The Histori-ography of the Rio de la Plata area since 1830," *ibid.*, XXXIX (November, 1959).

The Central American republics have often been convulsed by controversy between Church and state. A careful study of this issue in one of the republics is Mary P. Holleran, *Church and State in Guatemala* (New York, 1949). See also F. B. Pike, "The Catholic Church in Central America," *The Review of Politics*, XXI (January, 1959), and William J. Griffith, "The Historiography of Central America since 1830," *Hispanic Amer-ican Historical Review*, XL (November, 1960), which contains a valuable account of some of the polemical literature of Cen-tral America pertaining to the Church-state conflict.

Church and state in Brazil are discussed in William J. Cole-man, M.M., *The First Apostolic Delegation in Rio de Janeiro and Its Influence in Spanish America: A Study in Papal Policy, 1830-1840* (Washington, D.C., 1950), and Sister Mary Cres-centia Thornton, *The Church and Freemasonry in Brazil: A Study in Regalism* (Washington, D.C., 1948). The latter work contains much valuable background material, and judges Free-masonry in Brazil to have been decidedly anticlerical. The great Brazilian statesman Joaquim Nabuco, *Discursos parlamentares* (Rio de Janeiro, 1955), discusses the Church-state issue from an anticlerical point of view. An objective analysis is found in Roger Bastide, "Religion and the Church in Brazil," in Smith and Marchant, editors, *Brazil, Portrait of Half a Continent*. Thales de Azevedo, "Familia, Casamento e Divorcio no Brasil," *Journal of Inter-American Studies*, III (April, 1961), deals, in part, with the present-day influence of the Catholic Church. Stanley J. Stein, "The Historiography of Brazil, 1808-1889," *Hispanic American Historical Review*, XL (May, 1960), makes some references to the literature pertaining to the Church-and-state issue.

Some works that deal with Latin American Catholicism and touch upon relations between Church and state in more recent times are: William Crawford Barclay, *The Greater Good Neigh-bor Policy* (Chicago, New York, 1945); William J. Coleman, M.M., *Latin American Catholicism: A Self Evaluation* (Mary-knoll, N.Y., 1958); John J. Considine, M.M., *New Horizons in Latin America* (New York, 1958); Peter M. Dunne, S.J., *A Padre Views South America* (Milwaukee, 1945); John A. Mac-kay, *The Other Spanish Christ* (New York, 1930), containing some superb insights into and interpretations of Catholicism, as well as its critics and defenders, in Spain and Spanish America; Gustave Weigle, S.J., "A Theologian Looks at Latin America,"

The Review of Politics, XX (October, 1958). Valuable information on the role of the Catholic Church in today's socially explosive Latin America is contained in papers delivered at the 1963 University of Notre Dame Conference on Religion and Social Change which have been edited by William V. D'Antonio and Fredrick B. Pike and published in the volume *Religion, Revolution, and Reform: New Forces for Change in Latin America* (New York and Washington, 1964). Also useful are the *CIF Reports,* published ten times a year by the Center of Intercultural Formation in Cuernevaca, Mexico, and John J. Considine, M.M., ed., *The Church in the New Latin America* (Notre Dame, Ind., 1964). A highly informative series of pamphlets dealing with Protestantism in Latin America and its relations with the Catholic Church has been published, beginning in 1957, under the auspices of the National Council of Churches in New York City.

A monumental guide to Catholic missionary activity throughout the world, and tracing early missionary work in the American Hemisphere back to 1493 is Robert Streit, *Bibliotheca missionum,* 21 vols. (Munster, Aachen, 1916-1959). A useful bibliographical guide which contains occasional references to relatively recent publications dealing with the Catholic Church in Latin America is: S. A. Bayitch, *Latin America, a Bibliographical Guide* (Coral Gables, Fla., 1961). The cumulative editions of the *Handbook of Latin American Studies* are indispensable research guides. The twenty-third number of the Handbook, published in 1961, listed some three thousand entries selected from over thirty-five thousand available listings. The scholarly historical quarterlies *The Americas* and *Hispanic American Historical Review* contain reviews of new publications pertaining to Latin American history and related fields. Two valuable guides to the latter journal have been published: Ruth Latham Butler, editor, *Guide to the Hispanic American Historical Review, 1918-1945* (Durham, N.C., 1950), and Charles Gibson, editor, assisted by E. V. Niemeyer, *Guide to the Hispanic American Historical Review, 1946-1955* (Durham, 1958). The *Hispanic American Report,* published monthly at Stanford University, provides a detailed coverage of current news events in Spain, Portugal and Latin America. In addition, it lists many and reviews some of the recent publications pertaining to these areas.

A NOTE ON THE TYPE

THIS book is set in *Electra*, a Linotype face designed by W. A. DWIGGINS. This face cannot be classified as either modern or old-style. It is not based on any historical model, nor does it echo any particular period or style. It avoids the extreme contrasts between thick and thin elements that mark most modern faces, and attempts to give a feeling of fluidity, power, and speed.

Composed, printed, and bound by
Colonial Press Inc., Clinton, Mass.

BORZOI BOOKS ON LATIN AMERICA

Under the general editorship of Lewis Hanke,

COLUMBIA UNIVERSITY

THE CONFLICT BETWEEN CHURCH AND
STATE IN LATIN AMERICA*
Edited by Fredrick B. Pike

THE MASTERS AND THE SLAVES (ABRIDGED)
A STUDY IN THE DEVELOPMENT OF BRAZILIAN CIVILIZATION
By Gilberto Freyre

DO THE AMERICAS HAVE A COMMON HIS-
TORY? *
A CRITIQUE OF THE BOLTON THEORY
Edited by Lewis Hanke

AMAZON TOWN
A STUDY OF MAN IN THE TROPICS
(*With a New Epilogue by the Author*)
By Charles Wagley

A VOYAGE TO SOUTH AMERICA (ABRIDGED)
By Jorge Juan *and* Antonio de Ulloa
(*With an Introduction by Irving A. Leonard*)

AGRARIAN REFORM IN LATIN AMERICA
Edited by T. Lynn Smith

THE BANDEIRANTES *
THE HISTORICAL ROLE OF THE BRAZILIAN PATHFINDERS
Edited by Richard M. Morse

DICTATORSHIP IN SPANISH AMERICA
Edited by Hugh M. Hamill, Jr.

THE ORIGINS OF THE LATIN AMERICAN
REVOLUTIONS, 1808-1826 *
Edited by R. A. Humphreys *and* John Lynch

THE EXPULSION OF THE JESUITS FROM
LATIN AMERICA
Edited by Magnus Mörner

THE MONROE DOCTRINE *
ITS MODERN SIGNIFICANCE
Edited by Donald Marquand Dozer

A DOCUMENTARY HISTORY OF BRAZIL*
Edited by E. Bradford Burns

BACKGROUND TO REVOLUTION *
THE DEVELOPMENT OF MODERN CUBA
Edited by Robert Freeman Smith

IS THE MEXICAN REVOLUTION DEAD? *
Edited by Stanley R. Ross

FOREIGN INVESTMENT IN LATIN AMERICA*
CASES AND ATTITUDES
Edited by Marvin D. Bernstein

* Also available in a hardbound edition.